CASTRO

A BEGINNER'S GUIDE

CASTRO

A BEGINNER'S GUIDE

SEAN CONNOLLY

Hodder & Stoughton

A MEMBER OF THE HODDER HEADLINE GROUP

Orders: please contact Bookpoint Ltd, 130 Milton Park, Abingdon, Oxon OX14 4SB. Telephone: (44) 01235 827720, Fax: (44) 01235 400454. Lines are open from 9.00–6.00, Monday to Saturday, with a 24-hour message answering service. Email address: orders@bookpoint.co.uk

British Library Cataloguing in Publication Data
A catalogue record for this title is available from the British Library

ISBN 0 340 84620 8

First published 2002
Impression number   10 9 8 7 6 5 4 3 2 1
Year   2007 2006 2005 2004 2003 2002

Copyright © 2002 Sean Connolly

Cover photo from Bettman/Corbis
Typeset by Transet Limited, Coventry, England.
Printed in Great Britain for Hodder & Stoughton Educational, a division of Hodder Headline Plc, 338 Euston Road, London NW1 3BH by Cox & Wyman, Reading, Berks.

CONTENTS

Who is Fidel Castro?

Just over 145 kilometres (90 miles) south of the hot dog stands, skateboarders and windsurfers of Key West, Florida, lies a hotbed of communism. It opposes American foreign policy, pours scorn on **civil rights** in the United States and even offered to send in observers to monitor the Florida recounts during the ill-fated US presidential election in 2000. This 'David', which delights in taunting the Yankee 'Goliath' to the north, is Cuba. And standing at the helm of the Cuban communist government, as he has for more than four decades, is the tall, bearded figure of Fidel Castro.

REBEL WITH A CAUSE

Since he led a band of loyal **guerrillas** to power in 1959, Castro has governed this Caribbean island-nation through the force of his personality. Once a tropical backwater with huge gaps between rich and poor – and riddled with organized crime – Cuba has become a beacon for many other Third World countries. Nearly 100 per cent of the Cuban population can read and write. Life expectancy, at 76 years, is the highest in Latin America and patients from around the world are attracted by Cuba's state-of-the art eye surgery techniques. All of these advances, Castro tells Cubans in impassioned speeches lasting up to four hours, are thanks to the revolutionary zeal of the people.

Transforming Cuban society has not been clear sailing for Castro, or for the Cubans themselves. The **Marxist** ideology that underpins Cuba's communist system offers little scope for protest and dissent. Private companies, both Cuban and foreign-owned, were nationalized soon after Castro seized power. Cuba has no legal Opposition, and those who have questioned Castro's authority – including anti-communists, religious leaders and civil rights activists – have paid the price in long prison sentences and sometimes execution. During his time as commander-in-chief, Castro has sent military advisers and troops to support Marxist rebellions in other Third World countries – further antagonizing the United States and its allies.

DAVID AND GOLIATH?

Fidel Castro aligned Cuba with the Soviet Union during the height of the Cold War, and Cuba was the scene of two memorable episodes in the deadly US–Soviet rivalry. The first was the Bay of Pigs **debacle** of 1961, when

KEYWORD

Debacle: an action that is a complete failure.

the United States armed and transported 1300 anti-Castro Cuban exiles for an invasion of the island. The invasion was a total failure and it gave Castro the chance to paint the United States as a bullying brute. The second incident, just over a year later, is now remembered as the Cuban Missile Crisis and it brought the world to the brink of nuclear war. The Soviet Union, faced with US threats, was compelled to remove missiles that it had installed in Cuba. The United States won that particular showdown, but it became clear that there was trouble – in the form of Castro – in its own backyard.

Over the years the United States and its Central Intelligence Agency (CIA) have grown impatient to see the demise of Castro. Code-named, with no real sense of secrecy, 'the Beard', Castro has allegedly been targeted in up to 30 CIA-related assassination attempts. The weapons used in these attempts have ranged from the obviously deadly – bombs and high-power rifles – to the comical. Castro did not fall for the 'exploding cigar trick' in the early 1960s, although one of his close aides has admitted that Castro was nearly killed with a cyanide milkshake in 1964. The cyanide capsule froze and the terrified operative could not pour its contents into the milkshake.

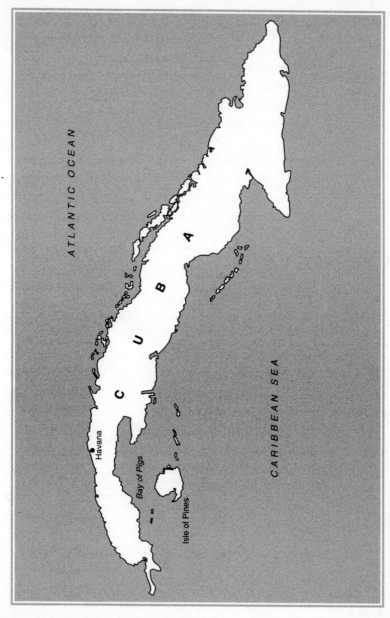

Cuba, the largest island in the Caribbean Sea.

Since these early conflicts with the United States, Fidel Castro has had to tread a fine line between asserting Cuba's independence and taking care not to push the United States too far. He gains enormous support within Cuba and abroad by playing up the 'David and Goliath' parallels. Castro stretched American tolerance by sending Cuban troops into Africa in the 1970s, but he chose not to risk doing the same when Marxist guerrillas were operating closer to home in Central America. Castro's response to the 11 September terrorist attack on New York was typical. He condemned the action as cowardly and expressed sympathy for the families who had lost loved ones. Then he went on to suggest that the real cause of the attack was American policy in the Middle East, which had driven the terrorists to such extreme measures.

KEY FACT

Big Brother is Watching

Rightly or wrongly, the United States has long considered Cuba to be part of its 'back yard', and it has treated Cuba like a headstrong child. It helped Cuba throw off Spanish colonial rule at the start of the twentieth century, but it prevented Cuba from achieving complete independence. American businessmen and criminals flooded into Cuba, which they considered to be something of a playground. By the time of the Revolution, American interests controlled a huge portion of the Cuban economy – and Cuban life in general. That is why the guerrillas did not seem to be a threat. As one American historian, Terence Cannon, wrote: 'The United States did not send in the marines for one basic reason: it did not fear the Revolution. It was inconceivable to the US policy makers that a revolution in Cuba could turn out badly for them. After all, US companies owned the country.'

The companies are long gone but the American presence continues on the island. The United States has military bases in Guantanamo, on the eastern tip of Cuba. Spain granted these to the United States in 1902 and America retains them as a way of keeping an eye on Castro's Cuba.

MARXISM AND SUGAR CANE

KEY FACT

What is Marxism?

The term 'Marxism' refers to the work and legacy of Karl Marx (1818–83), a German political philosopher whose work had a profound influence on world events. Marx developed the ideas that led to the notion of communism. He and his colleague Friedrich Engels (1829–95) observed working conditions in their native Germany and also in England. In their view, real power lay in controlling the means of production, or the way in which things got done. Nineteenth-century Germany and England had capitalist systems in which wealthy factory owners used money (or 'capital') to control the way in which their labourers worked and lived generally. This form of economic life would give way, they argued, to a fairer system in which the workers themselves had power. Marx called this system communism, taking its name from the same root as the word 'community'. The change might come overnight in the form of a revolution or capitalism might go through the halfway stage of socialism, which had some elements of each. Marx's most influential publication was the *Communist Manifesto*, with its famous rallying cry: 'Workers of the world unite! You have nothing to lose but your yokes.'

Since the very early 1960s, Fidel Castro's Cuba has operated under a Marxist form of government. Most of the restrictions – and idealistic goals – of Cuban society are linked to this political philosophy. Through most of the

KEYWORD

Manifesto: a public statement of beliefs.

40 years since Fidel Castro assumed power, Cubans have not been able to have private businesses or own more than a small amount of land. The government has been the major landowner and employer, with little scope for individual freedom. Under a Marxist system, central (government) planning dictates nearly every aspect of everyday life: where shops and schools will be built; how many doctors there should be in a neighbourhood or village; how many tonnes of each crop must be harvested each year. There is free education and health care, as well as low-cost housing, but the cost is high in terms of personal liberty.

In this respect Cuba in the 1960s and 1970s resembled Eastern Europe of the same period, with functional but ugly housing surrounding each city and huge banners urging people to produce more. Committees for the Defence of the Revolution (CDRs), a form of local **militia**, ensured that people worked hard and no one stepped out of line. But no matter how strictly Cuba interpreted its Marxist textbook, the

KEYWORDS

Militia: a body of citizens enrolled for military service.

Machete: a broad-bladed knife used to cut down sugar cane and other vegetation.

Caribbean island has always retained a character of its own. One of the qualities that has kept Cuba from being boring and monotonous has been the bold example of its leader. When hurricanes wrecked farms in the first years of the Revolution, Fidel rolled up his sleeves and joined in the bailing, rebuilding and rescue efforts. Some years later, when the government had set a difficult target for the sugar harvest, Castro was once more in the fields, hacking away with his **machete**. His style has always been to lead from the front.

Sugar was – and remains – the mainstay of the Cuban economy. Castro recognized this fact and made farming reform a priority as soon as he gained power. So it came as a blow to Castro when the United States, angry about the direction of the Cuban Revolution, stopped buying Cuban sugar in 1960. The Soviet Union, America's main rival in that Cold War period, stepped in to buy Cuba's sugar. From that point onwards, Castro found his room to manoeuvre lessened. He was limited, as ever, by the strength of each sugar harvest and also by the terms upon which the Soviet Union would buy the sugar. Each of these influences could be unpredictable, so it is something of a miracle that Cuba has remained so steadfastly independent.

MAXIMUM LEADER

Fidel Castro is the longest-serving head of government in the world, apart from Queen Elizabeth II of the United Kingdom. Although Castro lacks the regal touch, he has infinitely more power than the

Queen. From the moment Fulgencio Batista resigned as Cuban leader on 1 January 1959, it was obvious who would ultimately lead Cuba into the future. Real power lay in the hands of Castro and those aides whom he trusted. As the decades have drawn on, Castro has had an assortment of titles to reflect this power – commander-in-chief, prime minister, president of the state council. These titles change according to circumstances, but ordinary Cubans prefer to refer to Fidel Castro as *El Lider Maximo* ('The Maximum Leader'). The title seems to fit the man.

✱ ✱ ✱ *SUMMARY* ✱ ✱ ✱

● Fidel Castro led a band of guerrillas to victory in 1959 and has ruled Cuba ever since.

● Castro's Cuba is an example for many developing countries with its success in health and education.

● Cuba aligned itself with the Soviet Union soon after the Revolution, incurring the wrath of the United States.

● America responded by trying to assassinate Castro in order to overthrow his regime.

● Cuba was at the heart of two Cold War events: the Bay of Pigs attack in 1961 and the Cuban Missile Crisis of 1962.

● Since that time Fidel Castro has maintained his independence of the United States, often running great risks.

● Cuba has a Marxist government, which aims to produce equality although many individual freedoms are lost.

● Unlike other Marxist leaders, Fidel Castro has always led by example and joined the people in their labour.

● Fidel Castro has recognized the central role of sugar to Cuba's economy and he has tried to get the best deals for each harvest.

● Castro's unofficial, but appropriate title is 'El Lider Maximo' (the Maximum Leader).

2 Rebellious Youth

Cuba, the largest island in the Caribbean Sea, was ruled by Spain for more than four centuries. Christopher Columbus had landed there on one of his voyages to the 'New World' and the Spanish laid the first stones of the capital, Havana, before the start of the sixteenth century. The city, with its fabulous **baroque** architecture, grew and prospered. It was an important shipping centre for transporting gold and silver from Spain's American colonies.

WEALTH FROM SUGAR

It was not simply the capital that thrived during the colonial period. The island itself, with its fertile soil and ample sunshine, proved to be ideal for growing the most important crop in the Caribbean region – sugar cane. Sugar became the **cornerstone** of the Cuban economy, with most of the crop grown on large plantations. As was the case on neighbouring Caribbean islands, the landowners brought many African slaves to work the fields. Natural setbacks such as droughts and hurricanes could ruin a harvest, but the crop itself was so valuable that landowners soon regained what they lost.

The landowners formed the wealthiest class within Cuban society. They spent their money lavishly, building great mansions, spacious parks and attending grand balls and the opera. This way of life carried on after Cuba gained its independence in 1902. It was into this class that Fidel Castro was born in 1926. It was hardly the background one would expect for a guerrilla warrior and revolutionary, but Fidel was not the typical pampered heir to a sugar fortune.

ROUGH AND TUMBLE

For one thing, the Castro fortune did not stretch back generations. Fidel's father Angel was born into a poor family in north-western Spain, and he joined the army as a way of finding steady work. He was part of the force that Spain had sent to combat the Cuban rebels, and although Spain lost the conflict Angel stayed on to make a new life in Cuba. He worked hard, taking a range of jobs that included selling lemonade and working on the railway line. By saving hard, Angel Castro was able to buy a lumber mill and with these new earnings he leased more and more land. Eventually he controlled an estate of more than 10,000 hectares (24,700 acres) near the eastern city of Santiago. Much of the land was devoted to Cuba's biggest money-making crop – sugar.

The Castro estate was like a small town. It had its own store, post office, hotel, schoolhouse and small shacks for the migrant workers. Life was noisy, with constant fights and laughter. Workers, tired from the day's exertions on the sugar fields, would drink rum, play guitars and sing Cuban folk songs or gamble away their earnings by betting on cockfights. Fidel was not shielded from this life. As the fifth of nine children, he was also accustomed to noisy mealtimes and constant arguments. As a boy, Fidel showed signs of the large and powerful man he would be in later life. He put his size and strength to good use, excelling in baseball, swimming and athletics. Learning his lessons in the one-room schoolhouse along with the plantation workers' children, he showed great promise, although he hated any sort of authority.

Fidel was six years old when he was sent to the Catholic La Salle School in Santiago. His determination and already ferocious temper landed him in trouble as he argued with teachers and fellow pupils constantly. After three turbulent years at La Salle, Fidel enrolled at Dolores, another Catholic school in Santiago. This school was run by Jesuits. This highly disciplined Catholic order prizes self-reliance and debating skills. Fidel was in his element, soaking up names and dates in lessons while demonstrating his leadership skills on the playing field.

These sporting skills also helped Fidel socially. His rough manners and accent marked him out as a country boy, the sort who could easily fall victim to bullying by the wealthier town-dwellers who attended the school. Fidel would have none of that, and his athletic skills, muscular build and fiercely competitive spirit silenced anyone who stood in his way.

STUDENT OF HISTORY

The most powerful influence on the young Fidel Castro came from books as well as debates in class. He was fascinated by geography, politics and history – especially the military history of his own country. Fidel admired the great generals of history, such as Alexander the Great, **Hannibal** and Napoleon Bonaparte. He believed that such strong individuals were not only brilliant military commanders, but forceful characters who could shape the course of history itself. In

> **KEYWORDS**
>
> **Hannibal:** a general (247–183BC), of ancient Rome's enemy Carthage, who crossed the Alps and invaded Italy.
>
> **Elite:** representing the minority of society that has the best advantages (of wealth, education, etc.).

Fidel's view, Cuba had its own great figure in the form of José Martí (1853–95), but many Cubans, including Fidel himself, came to believe that Marti's work was unfinished since the United States still had such a stake in the country.

Fidel Castro's schoolboy years in Santiago also gave some glimpses of the dramatic gestures that would make him so famous – and feared – in later life. Fired with enthusiasm for the plight of workers, Castro tried to organize a strike among his father's labourers when he was only 13. A year later he wrote a letter of congratulations to US President Franklin Roosevelt, who had been elected to serve a third term of office. The school displayed the response (from the State Department, not the president himself) on its notice board.

So it was hardly surprising that Fidel was able to hold his own when he entered another Jesuit school, the **elite** Belin School in Havana. Once more Castro was surrounded by boys from privileged backgrounds, although in this school many of the boys came from Spain and looked down on any Cubans, no matter how well off. And once more Fidel threw himself into sports, devoting himself to baseball and basketball. Denied a place at first on the school basketball team, Fidel badgered the coach until he was allowed to take part. In no time he became captain. To add a finishing touch, in 1944 Fidel was named Cuba's best school sportsman for the year 1943–44.

All that sport meant that Fidel had little time for classwork or studying, but he used his exceptional memory to cram for exams, which he passed with distinction. When Fidel left school in 1945 his head wrote: 'He has known how to win the admiration and affection of all.'

KEY FACT

Cuban Independence

José Martí (1853–95) was Cuba's greatest patriotic hero and his life became an example for Fidel Castro. Like many Cubans in the nineteenth century, Martí hated Spanish colonial rule and decided to press for Cuban independence. His views brought a fierce reaction from the Spanish rulers, and he fled to the United States where he gathered a band of followers. Martí founded the Cuban Revolutionary Party, which became a government in exile at its New York headquarters. He argued that the only type of revolution that could succeed would be a guerrilla war with the support of the people, and that the same ordinary people should benefit directly, particularly in education and land reform. Martí also believed that the United States would eventually try to control Cuba and he urged Cubans to prevent such an outcome.

Martí launched what was to be Cuba's successful war of independence on 29 January 1895 and in March rowed ashore on the eastern coast of Cuba to join guerrillas who had assembled. Martí's short life ended on 19 May when he was shot by Spanish troops in combat. His guerrillas continued the struggle and, in 1898, the United States joined in the war against Spain after one of its battleships was blown up in Havana harbour. American involvement tipped the balance and the Spanish soon surrendered. Spain agreed to American control over the island, confirming Martí's fears. Cuba became an independent republic in 1902, but the United States imposed strict limits on Cuba's ability to conduct its own affairs.

José Martí was an inspiration to later Cuban revolutionaries, including Fidel Castro.

POLITICS AT UNIVERSITY

Fidel Castro enrolled in the Law Faculty of Havana University in October 1945. Despite his unusual method of studying, he had had a good education up to that point. The Jesuits had taught him to attack problems using logic and then pursuing each question to its inevitable conclusion. The University, however, was another matter. In some ways it was a mirror image of Cuba as a whole and in other ways it was a law unto itself. But one thing it lacked was a sense of academic discipline.

Professors were often appointed because of their political, rather than academic, qualifications. They had little interest in teaching and the students themselves knew they could buy exam papers. The trade in illegal papers was controlled by armed gangs of 'students' who were often in their 30s. President Grau San Martín turned a blind eye to the work of the armed thugs and even rewarded some with senior police posts.

KEY FACT

Political Turmoil

Cuba underwent a series of major political changes while Fidel Castro was at school and university. It lurched from democracy to dictatorship and back again, leaving ordinary Cubans bewildered and dissatisfied. President Gerardo Machado, elected in the 1920s as a progressive president, had become a dictator when the economy turned sour during the Great Depression. He suspended Cuba's constitution and used death squads to attack anyone who opposed him. The United States forced Machado to resign in 1933, replacing him with a more liberal regime.

Cubans, however, resisted this foreign-imposed government. Students teamed up with a wing of the military led by Sergeant Fulgencio Batista to overthrow that government in 1933. The new leader, Professor Ramón Grau San Martín, promised sweeping reforms but these threatened the interests of American companies in Cuba. Batista got American approval to topple Grau. He took over but promised to restore democracy. He gained a bit more independence from the United States and helped draft a new constitution which limited a president to one four-year term in office.

Cubans seemed to trust Batista when they elected him president in 1940, but by 1944 they had turned against military involvement in government. In elections that year Batista's chosen successor was defeated by Grau. This time, though, Grau showed little concern for social reform. Instead his government quickly gained a reputation for corruption and brutality. Meanwhile, armed gangs representing every shade of Cuban political opinion roamed the country freely.

Fidel Castro soon became aware of the turmoil in the university and the country at large. With his intelligence, physical size and powers of persuasion, he could have been a member of any of these gangs, but his independent spirit meant that he would not be satisfied following orders. He condemned the corruption and looked beyond the university for his political future. He found it as follower of Eddie Chibás, a rich congressman who founded a

KEYWORDS

Great Depression: the period in the 1930s when many countries faced economic hardship.

Constitution: the written code of laws that limits the power of a country's government.

new anti-corruption political party in 1947. As leader of this new Ortodoxo party, Chibás would run against Grau's successor, Prío Socarrás, in the 1948 presidential election.

Once more Fidel Castro found himself abandoning his studies for something more exciting, although this time it was politics rather than sport. He travelled widely trying to organize youth support and set up demonstrations for the Ortodoxo party. Many

KEYWORD

Bogota: the capital of the South American country, Colombia.

of these turned violent. He even joined in a short-lived attempt to overthrow the dictator of the Dominican Republic, Rafael Trujillo. In 1948 he was part of a group of South American students who travelled to Colombia. A renowned Colombian labour leader, Eliazar Gaitán, was assassinated while the group was in **Bogota**, leading to a full-scale rebellion against the government. Castro was in the thick of this revolt, riding through Bogota in a jeep. The police soon put down the revolt, and the Cuban group managed to leave Colombia without being charged with involvement.

The Colombian experience affected Castro immensely, and he could imagine similar scenes being played out on the streets of Havana. Although he described his presence in Colombia as 'accidental' and nothing to do with the revolt, he was on all the front pages of Havana's newspapers. He campaigned for Chibás in the June elections, but to no avail. Prío Socarrás won the election. No one was to know it then, but the election was to be Cuba's last.

Then Fidel Castro did something that surprised nearly everyone who knew him. On 12 October 1948, aged only 22, he married Mirta Díaz-Balart, a beautiful young philosophy student. They had had a brief courtship which Fidel managed to combine with his endless stream of meetings, demonstrations and speeches. His father-in-law was Batista's lawyer and had many connections within the political class that Castro was coming to despise. Within a year the couple had a young son, Fidelito ('little Fidel'). Fidel was hardly the ideal breadwinner: his studies had been interrupted and his political activities earned him nothing. Something had to be done – and soon.

❋ ❋ ❋ *SUMMARY* ❋ ❋ ❋

● Fidel Castro was born into a landowning family in 1926 although his father had earned – rather than inherited – his fortune.

● Life on the Castro estate was chaotic and lively.

● Fidel was educated by the Jesuits from the age of nine, first in Santiago and later in Havana.

● Sporting skills, physical strength and a powerful personality helped Fidel deal with teasing about his rural background.

● Although he often ignored his studies to play basketball and baseball, Fidel Castro got high marks in his final school exams after a brief period of intensive study.

● Fidel Castro entered Havana University in 1945, during a period when armed student gangs battled for political power.

● Castro was one of the first students to join the anti-corruption Ortodoxo party set up by Eddie Chibás in 1947.

● Fidel Castro was part of a group of Cuban students who took part in a short-lived revolt in Colombia in 1948.

● Prío Socarrás defeated Eddie Chibás in Cuba's last free presidential election in 1948.

● Fidel Castro married Mirta Díaz-Balart in October 1948 and their son Fidelito was born a year later.

3 The Politics of the Gun

With a family to support, Fidel Castro faced up to his responsibilities. He decided to complete his legal education in 1950. Typically, this involved cramming a two-year course into six months. He studied voraciously, choosing to read textbooks rather than attend classes. Even his political involvement dwindled as he concentrated on this single goal. He succeeded in September 1950 when he graduated from Havana University with the titles of Doctor of Law, Doctor of Social Sciences and Doctor of Diplomatic Law.

PRACTISING LAW

Castro set up a legal practice with two lawyers from poor backgrounds. He chose to concentrate on political cases and on furthering the aims of poor people. Typical cases involved defending market stallholders in Havana, peasants who faced evictions from their farms and students arrested for involvement with political protests. There were few fees to be collected from this work, and much of it fell under the category *pro bono publico* ('free public service'). This was not the way to become rich, but it was certainly a way to make a name. Castro's reputation grew considerably even during his first year as a lawyer.

Attacking the president

It was not enough for Castro merely to mount defences. He saw it as his responsibility as an increasingly well-known lawyer to go on the attack. His target was the president himself, Carlos Prío Socarrás. This was a potentially dangerous move, and Castro had taken the precaution of arming himself with evidence. In assembling five specific charges against the president, Castro enlisted the aid of the youth wing of the Ortodoxo party.

On 28 January 1952, he outlined these charges to a federal court. They included accusations that Prío had:

* accepted bribes in return for granting amnesty to a convicted sex criminal;

* forced workers into illegal 12-hour shifts;

* made soldiers perform excessively **menial** tasks;

* contributed to unemployment by using soldiers rather than allowing the unemployed a chance to earn a wage;

* betrayed national interests by selling farm products at below their **market value**.

Castro added to these accusations in February, but most importantly managed to have all of them published in the newspaper *Alerta* and broadcast on 'The Voice of Antilles' radio station. His profile was at an all-time high, and it seemed only natural that he turn this popularity to political advantage.

KEYWORDS

Menial: lowly and some-times degrading.

Market value: the price that something could fetch if it were sold freely.

Bourgeois: a Marxist term of abuse, referring to excessive devotion to private property.

CASTRO THE CANDIDATE

National elections were scheduled for June 1952. Castro intended to stand as an Ortodoxo party candidate for the chamber of deputies (Cuba's lower house), representing a Havana district. His profile was already high, with his investigation of the president and the publicized work on behalf of Havana's inner-city poor. Aware of the need to feed this publicity – and confident of his own eloquence – he made sure that his message got through on other levels.

Media assault

His preparations began in earnest more than a year before the election. Castro would have considered the Cuban political landscape at the time as **bourgeois**, yet he was able to manipulate it to his own advantage. In particular, he found ways to infiltrate the media at many levels in a way that would put modern-day US presidential candidates to shame.

Roberto Agramonte, the Ortodoxo presidential candidate, had an hour-long slot on the Havana radio station CMQ. Castro, however, thought that the party's youth – in the form of Fidel himself – should share that time. He succeeded in getting a weekly ten-minute section, which Agramonte agreed to give up. Another Havana radio station, Radio Alvarez, also gave Castro a regular slot and he used this to full oratorical effect. At the same time Castro continued to write occasional articles for *Alerta*, a newspaper that had proved itself to be a thorn in the government's side.

BATISTA SEIZES POWER

Fidel Castro never had a chance to stand in the June 1952 elections because Fulgencio Batista seized control of the government just as he had nearly 20 years before. The **coup** that consigned Castro's candidacy to history was

KEYWORD

Coup: a government take-over, often by force.

over almost as soon as it began. It had been planned meticulously and it had the crucial support of the armed forces. At dawn on 10 March 1952, Fulgencio Batista, accompanied by a core of high-ranking officers, simply walked into Camp Columbia in Havana. The army commanders at the base welcomed Batista and by 11 March he was already proclaimed Chief of State.

Political analysts today, with the benefit of hindsight, try to imagine Castro's career had the elections taken place. Many believe that Castro would have been elected and would have served in the chamber of deputies before aiming for the Senate and then – perhaps in 1960 or 1964 – standing for president.

What is certain is that Castro commanded enormous political support in 1952, especially among the youth section of the Ortodoxo party. Max Lesnick, the party's youth chief, remarked years later that Castro would certainly have been elected: 'I knew the influence he had among all the young people in the party, the most sincere people in the party, and the working people.'

Organizing the Movement

Batista represented nearly everything that Castro despised: landed interests, corruption and tolerance of organized crime, pro-business legislation and, most importantly, near-total obedience to the United States. This last point was to provide Castro with a powerful weapon throughout his revolutionary struggle and through the decades of his own rule.

In reality, Batista's coup and his subsequent rule were gifts for anyone who sought a **radical** overthrow of the existing system. In effect, Batista was removing the need to chip away within the system by underpinning his rule with military might. Castro, having learned of the coup, denounced Batista's 'brutal theft of

KEYWORDS

Radical: favouring drastic and wide-ranging changes.

Pragmatic: realistic and common-sense.

power' but within hours was planning an organized response. His strategy was twofold: to continue with his high-profile courtroom protests and street demonstrations while secretly organizing a Movement that would eventually overthrow the government.

The as-yet unnamed Movement relied on secrecy, using the 'cell' structure common to many revolutionary groups. Volunteers organized ten-member cells in a particular location, and each of those ten was to recruit another ten-member cell, and so forth. This approach reduced the number of contacts that any single member had. It also created a strong sense of loyalty. On a more **pragmatic** level, it meant that any arrested member would have relatively little information to disclose if arrested and tortured.

Safe as houses

Decades after the events, Castro explained that although he shared the political views of Cuba's Communist Party, he chose to 'go it alone'. The Communist Party had its own strongholds within Cuba's labour confederation, which had been tolerated by successive governments. They were reluctant to discard this semi-official status by embarking

on violent protests. Then, of course, there is
the personal element. Castro was a born leader,
and was unlikely to enrol in an organization
that would tie him to an intricate **bureaucratic**
structure.

Moreover, Castro had more immediate
concerns. His own personal safety – and by
extension that of the Movement – lay in
moving from place to place. Castro had slept at home on the night of
the coup, but left at dawn to go to the apartment of his sister Lidia. By
mid-morning, secret police had arrived at his apartment, proving that
his instincts were sound. Others in the Movement had worked behind
the scenes, finding a series of 'safe houses' where Castro could stay and
sleep over the following weeks. Most of these apartments belonged to
Castro supporters, or to other highly placed opponents of Batista.

KEYWORDS

Bureaucratic: (of an
organization) operating
with a rigid system of
rules and procedures.

Denunciation: a public
criticism.

THE PROPAGANDA OFFENSIVE

The next step was to publicize the aims of the Movement. Things had
changed overnight, however, after the coup and Castro was unable to
use his normal radio slots. Working secretly, he produced a
proclamation denouncing Batista, and he sent representatives to the
newspaper *Alerta*. The editors shied away from printing this new piece;
the new press censorship limited their freedom.

It was up to Castro to spread the word himself. He took 500 copies to
the Colon cemetery where Ortodoxo party leaders had gathered.
Hearing their luke-warm **denunciations** of Batista, he shouted: 'If
Batista grabbed power by force, he must be thrown out by force!' He
then distributed his proclamation copies. A week later he was even
bolder, returning to the courts in his role as lawyer and citing the
numerous ways in which Batista had violated the Constitution. He had
no hope of pursuing this legal attack successfully, but he knew that it
would be reported in the Press. It also offered a constitutional
justification for his later actions against the Batista government.

A PLAN OF ACTION

On 13 January 1953 Castro, along with several leading *Fidelistas* (as his followers were already known), attended a meeting of the Ortodoxo party. The meeting proposed an alliance with other anti-Batista political groups. This was too much for Castro, who already believed that the party's will to fight had been fatally weakened. He stormed out of the meeting.

Castro returned to his secret activities with renewed vigour. In his view, the time was right for an armed response to the illegal Batista government. The Movement gained a Military Committee, charged with training members in armed warfare as well as finding sources of weapons, many of which were stolen from police and army bases. Training took place in secret locations, with cell members from the university and the countryside assembling to practise manoeuvres. The aim, throughout early 1953, was to be ready to mobilize at an hour's notice for an armed action against Batista's forces.

Another anti-Batista group, known as the Nationalist Revolutionary Movement, had planned a similar violent action. Castro was asked to participate but declined on the grounds that it was too ambitious – to expect 50 men armed with pistols and knives to overthrow the army's most heavily armed camp. It was also a poorly guarded secret, another reason why the action failed dismally on 5 April. Castro was relieved to have played no part. Meanwhile Batista believed that the only real threat to his rule had been quashed.

ATTACK AND ARREST

Fidel Castro could never be accused of being half-hearted. In the one-year period after the coup he claimed to have driven 40,000 kilometres (25,000 miles) around Cuba, recruiting and supporting members of the Movement. His plans for a military uprising also reflected this devotion to detail. The aim was to attack Cuba's second-largest military base in Moncada, in the city of Santiago, well away from Havana. This region of Cuba was Castro's home turf, and he had spent many hours

exploring the remote Sierra Maestra mountains
back in the days when he was studying under
the Santiago Jesuits. With careful planning,
such as observing sentry patterns over a long
period, the attack would succeed with little or

KEYWORD

Arsenal: a weapons store-
house.

no bloodshed. A smaller base at Bayamo, about 140 kilometres (87
miles) north-west of Santiago, was to be overwhelmed in a similar
fashion in order to cut off military reinforcements. Then, established in
his own military base (and with a sizeable **arsenal**), Castro would be
able to summon national support through radio broadcasts. Batista's
support would crumble in the face of this two-pronged threat – one
military and the other at grass roots level.

In the event, things did not go quite as Castro had planned. Sixteen cars
carrying Castro and 121 armed attackers left a farm about 11
kilometres (7 miles) away from Moncada before dawn on 26 July 1953.
This train of cars was to burst past one of the Moncada gates allowing
the passengers to rush and disarm the sleeping soldiers. One of the cars
made a wrong turn, another got a flat tyre, and at the gate there were
more guards than originally foreseen. Instead of storming into the
base, Castro and his men were pinned behind parked cars exchanging
fire with a growing number of soldiers who had heard the alarm.
Castro stood firing at soldiers on the roof while his compatriots
scrambled to escape. Although Castro and some of his immediate aides
did survive Moncada, many others were killed or captured near the
base. The Bayamo operation had failed as well, with 12 rebels being
shot and ten escaping into the hills.

Over the next few days, Castro tried to regroup in the hills, aiming to
begin a long-running guerrilla campaign, but exhaustion and lack of
ammunition caused the group to dwindle, with individuals being
captured or shot outright by the pursuing military forces. The end
came at dawn on 1 August, when a 16-man rural guard squad came
across Castro's group and captured them.

'HISTORY WILL ABSOLVE ME'

The Batista regime needed to publicize its Moncada victory and in doing so exaggerated the extent of the threat, claiming that as many as 500 rebels had stormed the base. This image of military heroism was to be echoed in the trial of Castro and 121 other defendants, which began on 21 September 1953 in the Santiago Palace of Justice.

Batista had underestimated the way in which Castro would turn the trial into political theatre. Instead of defending their actions, Castro and his compatriots repeatedly denounced the regime. Asked who was the 'intellectual author' of the attacks, Castro replied that it was none other than José Martí, the hero of Cuban independence. The defendants made no effort to deny their part in the attack, and their candour meant that most of those who had not been directly involved could go free; 29 others were found guilty but received sentences far less than the maximum 20 years.

Castro's position was different. The authorities, embarrassed by his courtroom announcements, pretended that he was ill and continued his trial in a hospital room. In those bizarre surroundings, flanked by a human skeleton in a glass case, Castro made his now-famous defence speech. As his trial drew to a close, he was allowed to stand and make a speech in his defence. What followed was a two-hour *tour de force*, which painstakingly outlined the intellectual background of his actions, the illegitimate nature of the Batista regime and the unquenchable spirit of those Cubans prepared to fight for freedom. He concluded: 'Condemn me, it does not matter. History will absolve me.'

These last four words were to be the single defining element of the trial, overshadowing the 15-year sentence that Castro received. The date of the attack on Moncada (26 July) 'christened' the previously unnamed Movement.

✳ ✳ ✳ *SUMMARY* ✳ ✳ ✳

• Needing an income to support his family, Fidel Castro completed his law course and qualified in 1950.

• Castro became a high-profile lawyer, defending the poor and launching attacks on the president.

• Fidel Castro intended to stand as an Ortodoxo party candidate in the 1952 election.

• Using his powers of persuasion, Fidel Castro managed to get regular radio slots to make political broadcasts.

• A coup by Fulgencio Batista in March 1952 cancelled the June 1952 elections and Castro began organizing an underground Movement against the government.

• Castro shrewdly refused to take part in a poorly planned anti-government revolt which took place on 5 April 1953.

• Instead Castro travelled more than 40,000 kilometres (25,000 miles) around Cuba to build up support for his Movement.

• He planned to attack the Moncada army barracks in eastern Cuba, which would be the first step in an outright revolution.

• Bad luck and some planning mistakes caused the 26 July 1953 attack on Moncada to fail; Castro and other surviving guerrillas were arrested on 1 August.

• Castro's 'History Will Absolve Me' speech from the courtroom became a cornerstone of the Cuban Revolution, but did not prevent his conviction.

Guerrilla Victory 4

Fidel Castro and the other convicted revolutionaries began their prison sentences in the hospital wing of a new prison on the Isle of Pines off the south-western coast of Cuba. Conditions were not particularly difficult, and the group found they were treated as political prisoners. In practical terms, this arrangement meant that Castro and the other prisoners had a great deal of free time. They could correspond with people outside the prison and were able to cook their own food.

Never one to idle away his time – even on this tropical paradise island with its palms and cooling breezes – Castro set about educating himself and the other prisoners. He set up a school and established a disciplined routine with five hours of classes each day. These experiences, which were well recorded, served as an example for rebel leaders in other countries. Ten years later, and in considerably harsher surroundings, Nelson Mandela set up a similar school for his fellow African National Congress prisoners.

MEXICAN EXILE

These comfortable conditions came to a sudden end in February 1954, when Batista visited the jail. He was shocked when the Moncada rebels greeted him with a rousing revolutionary song. Castro was sent to solitary confinement, but he was still able to communicate with the outside world, rolling up secret letters in cigars and using invisible ink between the lines of letters that the guards would read. In this way, Castro smuggled out a copy of his speech 'History Will Absolve Me' – he had written it out completely from memory. This was a remarkable achievement. When later printed, the speech filled 54 closely printed pages. It took three months to smuggle out the entire text.

The speech was printed and circulated throughout Cuba, making Castro the most famous political prisoner in the country. His reputation grew further when the two women who had participated in the Moncada raid, Haydee and Melba Hernandez, were released later that same February. They added their voices to those of the prisoners' mothers to call for their release. Batista, meanwhile, felt that his

KEYWORD

Cadillac: an expensive American car, seen as a symbol of wealth.

own position was secure. More and more money was flowing in from the United States. A great deal of this money, however, was spent on gambling and prostitution so it did not help Cuba as a whole. The well-off were growing rich quickly, so much so that at one point Havana had more **Cadillacs** per head of population than any other city in the world.

With business booming, Batista decided to release his embarrassing prisoners, who only served to remind the world of the movement against him. Castro walked free on 15 May 1955. His release was headline news across Cuba, and Castro was not shy about vowing to return to his struggle. He reminded waiting reporters that the anti-government campaign now had a name, the 26 July Movement. This, of course, referred to the date of the Moncada attack. In the next few weeks, Castro made speeches, broadcast his opinions and wrote columns in newspapers and magazines. This was too much for Batista, who must have seen the mistake he had made in freeing Castro. The government turned on the publications that published Castro's articles, closing several of them outright and threatening the rest. Many of Castro's supporters were arrested and his friends feared for his life. Exile seemed to be the only answer, and on 7 July 1955 Fidel Castro flew to the safety of Mexico.

He left behind a message saying that all chance of a peaceful resistance had been closed to him. Referring to Batista as a dictator and accusing him of ruling by the use of terror and crime, Castro said that the hour had come for Cubans to demand their rights and not beg for them. He closed by referring to his temporary absence: 'From journeys such as this, a man either does not return or else returns with the tyranny dismembered at his feet.'

Although Castro's brother Raúl and a few friends had established themselves in Mexico a few weeks earlier, Fidel arrived with little money and few possessions. What he did have, though, was abundant confidence and the power of persuasion. And he had a plan. Castro sought out an ageing, Cuban-born soldier named Alberto Bayo who had fought in several guerrilla campaigns including the Spanish Civil War in the 1930s. He told Bayo that he expected to defeat Batista in a future landing with men 'when I have them' and with boats 'when I have the money to buy them'. Bayo was both amused and impressed. Most importantly, he was persuaded to train members of the 26 July Movement in how to conduct a long-term guerrilla war. He told Castro: 'The man of the guerrilla is invincible, provided he can rely on the support of the peasants in place.'

CHE JOINS THE MOVEMENT

Before leaving Cuba, Fidel Castro had told some of his friends of his plan to launch an attack from the sea. He had asked these friends to scout around the coast for the best location for a landing. It was important, he felt, that members of the Movement who remained in Cuba would have an idea of what he planned.

> **KEYWORD**
>
> Profit sharing: a system of business that allows all of a company's employees to benefit when the company does well.

Castro continued to communicate from Mexico with those in Cuba, using secret mail connections. Writing in a small rented room in Mexico City, he completed the 'Manifesto No 1 to the People of Cuba', a work that spelt out dozens of concrete proposals of how he would change Cuba. Among the most important were:

* the distribution of land among peasant families;

* an extension of electricity supplies;

* a drastic decrease of rents;

* the introduction of **profit sharing**;

* provision of day-care centres for the children of working families;

* wider access to health and education.

Castro worked hard to complete the Manifesto in time for the Congress of the Ortodoxo party in August 1955. He needed to build and maintain momentum for his 26 July Movement at home while he planned strategy in Mexico. New recruits joined the Movement while other groups also formed to overthrow the Batista government. The single most important recruit joined the Movement in Mexico, and he was not even Cuban. Raúl Castro introduced his brother to a young doctor named Ernesto 'Che' Guevara, who had left his native Argentina in 1953 to combat American dominance in Latin America. The two men – Che was slightly younger than Castro – recognized that their futures lay together. Che was a committed Marxist who soon began spending long hours discussing Cuba's future with Castro. A lifelong friendship developed between the two, and Che helped Fidel develop plans for the landing in Cuba.

Columbian author Gabriel García Marquez was impressed with Cuba's exiled guerrilla leader.

By the time Fidel Castro turned 30 in August 1956, the plans were well under way. Money was a worry, because the Movement needed to bribe the Mexican police in order to keep their plans secret. Castro visited Cuban exiles in the United States to raise money and look for recruits. One of the most willing was Camilo Cienfuegos Gorriaran, a young worker from Havana who had left for California after a skirmish with the police. By now the Movement had nearly a hundred volunteers in Mexico. Under Bayo's guidance they drilled each day near a farmhouse that Castro had bought with funds he had raised.

THE ORIENTE LANDING

Castro was desperate to launch the invasion before the end of 1956, but he needed to finish the planning for what would happen when the guerrillas arrived. He planned to land in the eastern province of Oriente. A series of disturbances and demonstrations elsewhere in Cuba would distract Batista's troops, allowing the guerrillas to make their way to mountain headquarters in the nearby Sierra Maestra. Frank País, the Movement's co-ordinator in Oriente, flew to Mexico and agreed to the plan. Then Castro met Jose Antonio Echeverría, the leader of Cuba's Student Revolutionary Directorate, which some people saw as a rival to the 26 July Movement. After long discussions Castro and Echeverría signed a pact in which they promised to work together after the landing.

The Movement had built up a supply of weapons in eastern Mexico. In late September, with the self-imposed deadline of the end of the year approaching, Castro bought a 56-year-old wooden yacht. Its American owner had named it the *Granma* after his grandmother.

Still thinking of his own deadline, Castro believed that he had nearly three months to prepare his men and the boat for the voyage. But things soon took on an unexpected urgency. On 22 November, Castro learned that some of his men had given themselves up to the Mexican authorities. They would no doubt be telling the Mexicans – and by extension, Batista – about the exact details of the voyage. The time had come to go. After sending a coded message to Frank País, Castro got his 81 men and supplies on board the *Granma*. In pouring rain on the night of 25 November they set off from the Mexican port of Tuxpan.

Castro had predicted a five-day voyage so that the landing would coincide with an uprising in Santiago led by Frank País, but bad weather and mechanical problems slowed the progress of the *Granma*. By the time Castro's guerrillas waded in to the muddy shore on 2 December they had missed the disturbances. They had also missed a rendezvous with a local bandit who would lead them to safety in the mountains.

UNSHAKEABLE CONFIDENCE

The rebels climbed to higher ground above the swamp and found a shack owned by Angel Perez Rosabal, who was the first person they met ashore. The rebel leader said: 'Have no fear, I am Fidel Castro. We come to **liberate** the Cuban people.' The statement was pure Castro – assertive and confident despite outward

> **KEYWORDS**
>
> Liberate: to set free.
>
> Garrison: a group of soldiers stationed in an armed building.

appearances. The truth was that the 82 rebels had no food, few weapons and no contact with the Movement on shore. Lined up against them were Batista's forces: combined troops numbering 40,000; armed National and Rural Guards; Sherman tanks; and a squadron of Cuban Air Force combat jets. Plus, the government learned of Castro's arrival within two hours of the landing.

With these odds, Castro's position seemed hopeless. To make matters worse, the rebels were ambushed and nearly wiped out three days after arriving. The 16 survivors, including Castro, scattered and regrouped in the hills of the Sierra Maestra. There they met other Movement rebels, but numbers were still low. Patiently and calmly Castro addressed the main problem of finding weapons. These came as a result of a daring raid on the **garrison** of La Plata on the coast. Castro's 27 guerrillas swept in and burned the barracks, carrying off all the weapons.

The following month Castro had a victory of a different kind. Herbert Matthews, a *New York Times* reporter, visited the rebel camp. Castro's men tricked Matthews into believing that their numbers were much larger. At one point a sentry rushed in with news of a second column of guerrillas (which did not even exist). Matthews wrote a lengthy article about the success and might of Cuba's rebel leader. The piece was reprinted in Cuba the following week and created a fervour of excitement among the people.

OVERTHROWING A DICTATOR

Gradually Castro gathered more guerrillas into his group, which remained in the impenetrable slopes and valleys of the Sierra Maestra. Meanwhile the public was becoming more and more restless. Batista's forces conducted a house-to-house search of Santiago for Frank País, whom they finally captured and executed in July 1957. There were huge demonstrations at his funeral, followed by a general strike. Rebel flags flew over buildings in Havana and other cities.

Each public demonstration strengthened Castro and weakened Batista. Castro had banked on public support, which was growing through 1957. Cubans were horrified by the violent behaviour of the police and armed forces as they hunted down rebels. The next breakthrough came in February 1958 when the guerrillas acquired a radio transmitter and began broadcasting from *Radio Rebelde* ('Rebel Radio'). Rebel raids gained more weapons and Echeverría's Revolutionary Directorate was stirring up constant protests in the cities. A general strike on 9 April 1958 confirmed the widespread anti-Batista feeling in the country. Castro began to get support from an unlikely assortment of sources: the Catholic Church, the Communist Party and even the United States. Although representing different points of view, they shared one belief: that Castro would succeed.

Batista, backed into a corner, tried one last attempt to crush the rebels. On 24 May 1958 he sent 7000 troops into the Sierra Maestra. General Eulogio Cantillo, the army commander, sent a message urging Castro to surrender. Castro's written refusal was confident but at the same time showed his respect for the general. The fighting continued for 76 days. Hounded every step of the way by sure-footed rebels, the soldiers failed in each attempt to capture the guerrilla stronghold.

The Batista regime began to unravel in late 1958, confronted by guerrilla successes. The rebels controlled a large portion of the island and Che Guevara had begun blockading several ports. Even Batista's main ally, big business, was abandoning him. On Christmas Eve 1958, General Cantillo met Castro personally. This time he offered to revolt and to turn the government over to Castro. Less than a week later, Fulgencio Batista left a low-key New Year's Eve party and boarded a plane for the Dominican Republic. His final act was to appoint General Cantillo as head of the armed forces.

✷ ✷ ✷ SUMMARY ✷ ✷ ✷

● The Moncada rebels began their prison sentences in comfortable conditions in a prison on the Isle of Pines.

● Castro set up a prison school with daily classes for his fellow prisoners.

● Despite a spell in solitary confinement, Castro smuggled out a copy of his famous speech 'History Will Absolve Me'.

● The Moncada prisoners were freed on 15 May 1955 after a campaign for their release by their mothers.

● Fearing for his life, Castro moved to Mexico where he began planning a landing to overthrow the Batista regime.

● Key contacts with a former guerrilla commander and his new friend Che Guevara helped Castro develop a disciplined core of rebels.

● Castro's band of 82 rebels landed in eastern Cuba on 2 December 1956.

● Although hopelessly outnumbered by government troops, Castro never lost confidence that he would succeed, and gradually this confidence spread to the Cuban public.

● Castro's rebels and their allies created a series of disturbances against Batista, winning military skirmishes and gaining a wide range of support from home and abroad.

● On New Year's Eve 1958, Fulgencio Batista fled Cuba and named General Cantillo as head of the armed forces.

Enemy Number One

5

With Batista gone, and with nearly all of Cuba celebrating his departure, the way was clear for a new government to meet the needs and demands of ordinary Cubans. The jubilant population of Havana smashed parking meters and gambling equipment and even broke the windows of American-owned hotels. But New Year's Day 1959 did not see the dawn of a new rebel government led by Fidel Castro. Instead, General Cantillo and other military leaders who had agreed to revolt, promising to turn the government over to Castro, now looked set to hold on to power.

The pattern was familiar to anyone who understood the unsettled nature of Latin American politics. A group of senior military leaders, or **junta**, takes power and declares itself to be the new government. The junta argues that it has acted in the national interest

KEYWORD

Junta: a group of military leaders who govern a country, usually by force.

by promising a swift return to law and order. Free and democratic elections, along with social reforms, might be promised, but the emphasis is on stability.

Fidel Castro, still far from the capital in his eastern stronghold of Santiago, might have been worried or discouraged by this possible course of events, but apart from his own immense self-belief, he knew he had another powerful weapon – the Cuban people themselves. From his earliest schooldays, Castro had taken a keen interest in military planning. The victories of Napoleon and Hannibal – not to mention the setbacks met by his own hero José Martí – were to provide vital lessons. One of the most important of these was the ability to distinguish between short-term tactics (to achieve an immediate goal) and longer-term strategies (to make good these advances and move on from them).

He kept his strategy – the exact nature of a new Cuban government – out of the public view. His tactics for dismantling the junta and gaining power were a different matter. Broadcasting as he had throughout the rebel campaign from *Radio Rebelde*, Castro denounced the junta leaders as '**accomplices** of tyranny'. To ensure that no new government could take power in Havana he called for a general strike. Cubans heeded this call and turned the strike into a joyous three-day holiday (1–3 January).

KEYWORDS

Accomplice: a person who knowingly helps someone else in a crime.

Entourage: a group of followers.

TRIUMPHANT WELCOME

Castro also ordered Che Guevara and Camilo Cienfuegos to march on Havana. They had to secure – by force if necessary – two important military centres there. In the event there was no need for violence. Most of the military, like the country as a whole, welcomed the chance for a clean break with the past. On New Year's Day the Havana bases were turned over peacefully to army officers who had been released from prison for having opposed the Batista regime. Guevara and Cienfuegos arrived in Havana on 2 January to find the capital in festive mood. There was no violence, only singing and chanting long into the night. And the name on everyone's lips was that of Fidel Castro.

That same day Fidel Castro and his **entourage** arrived in Santiago. They were met with outpourings of joy and relief. Always aware of the power of symbolism, Castro took possession of the Moncada Barracks where the revolution had been launched on 26 July 1953. That evening Castro addressed an enthusiastic crowd in Santiago – his first speech as victorious rebel leader. He named Manuel Urrutia as provisional President of Cuba. His speech also focused on a significant difference between 1959 and 1898, the year of the Martí-inspired revolution. Pointedly referring to US involvement in the previous revolution, Castro promised: 'This time it will not be like 1898, when the North Americans came and made themselves masters of our country.'

The speech set the tone for the hundreds of
other speeches that Castro would make as
leader over the next four decades. It was
inspiring, calling for sacrifices on the one hand
but praising the efforts of ordinary people on
the other. The people, he stated, would now be
able to carry on with the business left
unfinished by José Martí and the heroes of

KEYWORDS

Rhetoric: the ability to
use language effectively.

Cabinet: a group of senior
political aides who help
shape government policy.

1898. Castro's **rhetoric**, like his physical stature, seemed larger than life.
The enthusiastic crowds in Santiago were nothing compared to the
singing, cheering masses who greeted Castro when he arrived in Havana.
Riding in an open-topped jeep, dressed in battle fatigues and smoking a
choice Cuban cigar, Castro entered the city to the sounds of church bells
ringing, factory whistles blowing and ships' horns sounding.

SECURING REAL POWER

First impressions suggested that Fidel Castro seemed to be happy to be
on the sidelines. He retained the title of Commander-in-Chief of the
armed forces, but allowed President Urrutia to assemble a **cabinet**.
Behind the scenes, however, Castro was running the government from
his hotel suite in the Hilton Hotel where the secret Office of
Revolutionary Plans and Co-ordination met. He then presented his
plans to the public in long speeches and in television broadcasts. The
president and cabinet simply approved these plans without discussion.
On 13 February, this secrecy ended as Castro became prime minister.
Urrutia was still president, but his powers had dwindled to next to
nothing.

With his new powers, Castro was able to begin to set in motion some
of the economic and social reforms that he had cherished as ideals for
years. These included improved housing and medical care as well as
better education and working conditions for all Cubans. In order to
pay for the enormous cost of these plans, Castro proposed a socialist
government. The state, in the form of his government, would take over,
or nationalize, many of the largest companies and farming concerns.

Most Cubans welcomed these proposals, but there were many who had prospered under the Batista regime and who saw that they stood to lose out. Moreover, there were still many Cubans who had actually enforced some of the harshest of Batista's policies. Thousands of anti-Castro Cubans fled the country, making the short 145-kilometre (90-mile) trip to the United States. Even today, more than four decades after Castro's rise to power, they and their offspring still harbour a deep resentment against Castro and his regime. Those senior Batista officials who stayed behind were tried before revolutionary tribunals. About 500 of those convicted were executed by firing squad. Diplomatic and business representatives from the United States expressed their concerns about these trials, but Castro insisted that justice was being done and that the public was satisfied. In February, speaking as usual before thousands in central Havana, he asked what should be done with war criminals. As if with one voice they answered: 'To the wall!'. The trials continued.

Worries about the course of Cuban justice were not the only American concerns. The new wave of Cuban immigrants to the United States told of the harsh treatment they had received. They spoke of evictions and religious persecution. More ominously for the Americans, they told of Castro's increasing friendliness with the Soviet Union. This, of course, was all taking place in the depths of the Cold War, when the United States and its capitalist allies were at odds with the Soviet Union and its communist friends.

American concerns deepened later in 1959. On 16 July the Havana newspapers ran huge headlines saying 'Fidel Resigns!' The following day, in a television address, Castro announced that he had resigned his post as prime minister because he could no longer work with the

KEYWORD

Defector: someone who leaves a country to live in that country's main enemy country.

president. According to Castro, President Urrutia was conspiring against the revolution. Castro alleged that the president had sided with a prominent **defector**, Major Díaz Lanz, who had fled to the United

States and denounced the rising communist influence in Cuba. The president only learned of the accusation – and of Castro's resignation – while watching the broadcast. Knowing Castro's power over the people and having witnessed the severe **tribunals**, the horrified president resigned immediately and sought refuge in the Venezuelan embassy. On 26 July,

KEYWORDS

Tribunal: an organized meeting to decide on the fate of someone.

Unanimously: in complete agreement.

the anniversary of the revolution, Castro agreed to return to his post under a new president, the radical Osvaldo Dorticós.

THE INTERNATIONAL ARENA

Now working with a president whose views echoed his own, Castro found it easier to enact new laws smoothly. He retained and even cultivated his image of a guerrilla leader, with his recognizable beard, battle fatigues and peaked cap, but he passed on the responsibility for military matters to his brother Raúl. Castro's other close ally, Che Guevara, became minister for industry and head of the national bank. Fidel himself was able to concentrate on overall strategy and on maintaining the momentum of the revolution.

Castro was well aware of the areas where potentially dangerous protests might arise and one by one he sought to lessen these threats. University lecturers whose views might be interpreted as being anti-revolutionary found themselves without jobs. In October 1959, Castro showed up in person and persuaded students to vote **unanimously** for his candidate in the student union elections. There was also pressure on labour unions to choose pro-Castro leaders. Although Castro boasted that the Cuban Press remained free – unlike the position under dictators elsewhere in the world – newspapers were forced to print pro-government paragraphs at the end of any critical article. Those that refused were closed down, sometimes under threat of mob force. Cuba's nearest neighbour, the United States, viewed these events with concern and suspicion, but none of these measures provoked an American reaction as much as Castro's growing friendliness with the

Soviet Union. In February 1960, the Soviet Deputy Prime Minister, Anastas Mikoyan, opened a trade fair in Havana. More than a million Cubans attended – a point that impressed Castro. A great deal of behind-the-scenes diplomatic activity accompanied these relations and, in early 1960, Cuba announced that it would co-ordinate all its economic planning under one central plan, known as the *Juceplan*. This system was almost exactly that used in the Soviet Union and many people began to view Castro's Cuba as being communist in everything but name.

Relations between Cuba and the United States worsened in June 1960 when a shipment of Russian oil arrived in Havana. Che Guevara, in his role as minister for industry, ordered American oil companies in Cuba to refine it. When they refused he nationalized the companies. US President Dwight Eisenhower then cancelled imports of Cuba's most important crop, sugar. Soviet leader Nikita Khrushchev responded by increasing purchases of Cuban sugar in return for more Soviet oil. He also promised to help protect Cuba's independence, possibly even in military fashion. Cuba, in turn, was nationalizing more and more American companies.

By late 1960, the United States government had lost any shred of sympathy it had felt for the plucky guerrilla leader who had ridded his country of a corrupt dictator. Instead, Castro became a villain who was intent on giving America's chief enemy, the Soviet Union, a foothold in 'America's back yard'. On 13

KEYWORD

Blockade: either an actual blocking of ports by armed ships or a ban on trade with a particular country.

October, Eisenhower banned all American exports to Cuba except medicines. This was the beginning of America's economic **blockade** of Cuba. On 29 October, the United States withdrew its ambassador, signalling an end to diplomatic relations.

With economic and diplomatic ties with the United States broken, the way was left clear for something even more dramatic. Castro had

Fidel Castro enjoyed his hands-on role during the Bay of Pigs Invasion of 1961.

foreseen a possible invasion from the United States and in late 1960 had established Committees for the Defence of the Revolution (CDRs), which were like an informal national guard. His suspicions were borne out on 15–16 April 1961 when the new US President, John F. Kennedy, set in motion a plan to attack Cuban airfields and land 1500 anti-Castro troops at the Bay of Pigs on Cuba's south coast. Castro seemed to have had advance knowledge of the attack. He hid Cuba's best planes from the initial bombings and then used them to defeat the landing force. The event was a triumph for Castro, who denounced the Americans to resounding cheers from his people.

Privately, though, Castro and his inner circle still feared an invasion. In mid-1962 Raúl Castro made a trip to Moscow where he made a deal that led to Soviet defensive missiles being stationed in Cuba. By October, high-flying American spy planes had photographed Soviet freighters unloading atomic missiles in Cuba. This development infuriated the United States, which saw it as a virtual act of war on the part of the Soviet Union (using Cuba as a pawn). More Soviet ships were on their way, but President Kennedy announced that he was forming a blockade around Cuba and that any vessel passing through it would be attacked. Cuba's defence needs had triggered the worst crisis of the Cold War. The world waited anxiously for several days until the Soviet ships finally turned back.

* * * SUMMARY * * *

• Military leaders who helped depose Batista seemed poised to assume power in January 1962.

• Fidel Castro called for a general strike, which ended any fears of a military takeover.

• In his first speech as revolutionary leader, Castro named a well-respected moderate, Manual Urrutia, as the new president.

• Cheering throngs welcomed Castro and his inner circle into the capital, Havana, in the first week of 1959.

• Castro developed government strategy behind the scenes at first and then more openly once Urrutia resigned and was replaced by a more revolutionary president.

• New laws and government plans concentrated on nationalizing foreign (and largely American) companies as a way of paying for expensive reforms.

• These strategies, coupled with increasingly frosty relations with the United States, led Cuba to form a closer relationship with the Soviet Union.

• The United States had broken virtually all economic and diplomatic ties with Cuba by the end of 1960.

• Castro's prior knowledge of an American attack helped Cubans to repulse the Bay of Pigs invasion in April 1961.

• Cuba's concerns for its own defence led to accepting Soviet missiles, an action that caused a dramatic Cold War crisis in October 1962.

Tropical Marxism

By the early 1960s, Fidel Castro had overthrown the much-hated Batista regime and set in place a new, revolutionary government in Cuba. Despite the constitutional arrangements that defined roles for a president, prime minister and cabinet – suggesting that decisions would be reached jointly and after detailed debate – the real power lay with 'The Maximum Leader' himself. Castro knew that fundamental changes could only come about if the people believed that the country's leadership was decisive and confident. He also knew that the people recognized him as the natural leader, so those same leadership qualities would need to be applied to himself. He nurtured his image, appearing in public dressed in the battle gear that recalled his years as a guerrilla leader and military genius.

Castro also knew that his victorious settlement within Cuba had inflamed opinion against him beyond his own borders. In particular, the United States viewed Castro as a real threat. If a determined guerrilla leader had managed to establish a pro-Soviet state in one Latin American country, they argued, how many more would soon follow his example? Their suspicions seemed confirmed on 1 December 1961 when Castro declared: 'I am a Marxist-Leninist and shall remain so until the last days of my life.' Cuba's leader had thrown down the gauntlet. The revolution was, and would remain, Marxist.

REWORKING A PHILOSOPHY

It was significant that Castro used the term 'Marxist-Leninist' to describe his political philosophy. As we have seen, Karl Marx lived and wrote in the nineteenth century and had remained convinced that communist revolutions would first develop within the most industrial countries. He had in mind either Germany, his birthplace, or Great Britain where he lived for many years. Both of these countries had advanced industries relying on working-class labourers (the proletariat) living in great cities. It was this group of people he was addressing when he wrote 'Workers of the world unite – you have nothing to lose but your yokes.'

In the event, neither Germany nor Great Britain witnessed a Marxist revolution. The nation where Marxism did triumph was Russia, one of the least developed of all European nations. Guided by Vladimir Lenin,

KEYWORD

Blueprint: the basic plans for a grand design.

the Russian Revolution of 1917 took hold in a country where the vast majority of people lived on the land. Lenin argued that the proletariat would not be able to organize in such conditions. Instead, a disciplined core of revolutionaries would need to overthrow the existing regime on their behalf. Moreover, the same small group would need to secure the advances of the revolution and govern – again, on behalf of the workers. It was this concentration on the 'core of revolutionaries' that marked Lenin's refinement of the Marxist doctrine. Although born out of a need to work within Russia's unique conditions, the strategy became the **blueprint** for later Marxist revolutionaries. Mao Zedong (1893–1976), China's leader, had applied Marxist-Leninist techniques to secure and maintain a communist victory in 1949 and thereafter.

Castro saw that this pragmatism could be applied to his own country. Like Russia and China, Cuba had no real tradition of heavy industry. Castro concluded that Cuba's revolution would also need the guidance of a devoted core. From his earliest schooldays, he had admired great individuals who shaped the course of history. Lenin's concern with individuals, rather than relying on Marx's theoretical 'inevitable victory' of the workers, sat well with Castro's understanding of how things worked in real life. Cuba was his to mould.

SUPERPOWERS AND SUGAR
Having proclaimed himself a Marxist-Leninist, Castro needed to create a system that worked in Cuba. No matter what political system was in

place, the people needed to believe that it suited their country and their own needs. So throughout the 1960s, as the Revolution needed to find its feet and gain acceptance at home, Castro adopted two strategies. The first reflected Castro's understanding of international politics during this tense period of the Cold War. The second, which tied in with this international view, concentrated on life within Cuba.

On the international front, Castro skilfully turned America's wrath and threats into something positive. He reasserted Cuba's need to be free from US interference. The defeat of the Bay of Pigs attack in 1961 became a propaganda triumph, since it showed America's aggressive intentions while at the same time displaying the pluck and courage of the ordinary Cubans who helped in the victory.

Having failed to overthrow Castro in armed conflict, the Americans, allegedly, considered assassination. America's Central Intelligence Agency (CIA) had many such schemes, including using an exploding cigar, poisoning his scuba-diving wetsuit and adding poison to his milkshake. Castro's instincts and his intelligence services – not to mention the silliness of some of the plans themselves – helped the Cuban leader escape danger. The effect of the CIA plans was to strengthen Castro's anti-Americanism. To this day, Cuban billboards depict Uncle Sam as scheming and evil, and *Yanquis* ('Americans') are the bogeymen intent on crushing the spark of Cuban independence.

Upsetting the Americans, coupled with Castro's own developing political philosophy, meant drawing closer to the Soviet Union. Even in this relationship Castro was his own man. He knew that Cuba relied on its steady

KEYWORD

Embargo: a government order prohibiting trade.

trade with the Soviet Union because of the trade **embargo** mounted by the United States and its allies. He also knew the value (to Moscow) of having a friend so close to the United States. That gave him strength in dealing with the Soviet Union. Castro was never afraid of speaking his mind and at times upsetting Cuba's new friends. When Soviet Premier

Nikita Khrushchev backed down during the Cuban Missile Crisis of October 1962, Castro flew into a rage, smashing furniture and breaking a mirror in his official residence, and during an official visit to the Soviet Union.

Things were on a more even footing in 1963 when Castro began a 40-day stay in the Soviet Union. The visit highlighted the Cuban leader's independent spirit and his 'common touch'. During his stay, he upset Soviet government officials by going on an unscheduled

KEYWORD

May Day: 1 May, the most important holiday in Marxist countries as it celebrates labour.

'walkabout' in Red Square, greeting ordinary Russians and behaving much as he would in Havana. This behaviour paid off when Castro was reviewing the traditional **May Day** Parade from the Kremlin. The public welcomed him more enthusiastically than any visiting leader since World War II. The grey-coated Soviet officials, normally aloof and sombre on these occasions, benefited simply by standing near the fiery guerrilla leader. The Soviet leaders acknowledged this the following year by offering Cuba a generous trade deal: buying Cuban sugar for a high price and selling oil to the Cubans cheaply.

It was vital for Castro to maintain both strands of his foreign policy – side-stepping the Americans while working the Cuban–Soviet relationship to his own advantage – in order to succeed at home. And that is where the Cubans began to see some real improvements to their lives. One of the central planks of Marxist government is central planning. Every aspect of a country's economy is dictated by the government. Castro followed the Soviet example in this area, but he was careful to concentrate on major problems in turn. Each year had its name: 1961, for example, was the Year of Education. Castro's target was to end illiteracy in Cuba and over the course of the year some 10,000 classrooms were built across the country. Students dispersed into rural districts where peasant children learned to read and write. The approved text for this course, *Venceremos* ('We will succeed') had a decidedly political flavour. The first words to be learnt included *Fidel, Raúl, Cuba* and '*La Reforma Agraria*' ('**Agrarian** Reform'). Successful pupils could then move on to their first sentence: 'The peasants work in the **co-operative**.'

Other years focused on health, medicine and so forth, but the early references to agrarian reform and co-operatives showed a theme that

KEYWORDS

Agrarian: referring to farming and agriculture.

Co-operative: a farming or business group in which people pool their talents and skills and share any profits from goods they produce and sell.

ran through all of Cuba's economic planning. Castro recognized that the country depended crucially on sugar, as it had for centuries. A series of land reforms in the early 1960s reduced the amount of land that an individual could own, and Castro intended to turn the whole farming sector into co-operatives by the end of the decade. In the meantime there were targets for the annual sugar harvests. Typical harvests in this period – the early 1960s – were 3–4 million tonnes. In 1963, Castro announced that the harvests would increase through the decade until they reached a target of 10 million tonnes by 1970. Such a massive increase would involve lots of 'voluntary' work, as city dwellers would join rural farmworkers in the fields over weekends and during holidays.

A NATIONAL FOCUS

As Cuba edged towards a Marxist form of government, ordinary Cubans saw a number of gains, notably free health care and education and guaranteed employment. These soon translated into living conditions that were the envy of most Third World nations. The price to pay for these improvements came in a steady loss of certain freedoms – to own land, to run private businesses, to have a free Press and to travel freely. Throughout this period Castro was careful not to copy the example of the Soviet Union too closely, and he insisted that Cuba's identity and special needs were the basis for the Revolution and government. He saw his role as focusing the needs of the people into sensible planning. In his first few years in power, Castro would ride through the countryside in his open-top Jeep, stopping to ask people what they thought was good and bad about the state of the country. Policies were decided 'on the hoof' at times, reflecting the need to respond to specific crises rather than follow an official Marxist blueprint. It is significant that the Cuban Communist Party was only created in late 1965, nearly seven years after the Revolution.

Unlike the Soviet rulers, who seemed remote from the people and set unachievable goals in farming and industry, Castro was willing to roll up his sleeves and join in – and in hard times he was seen even more. When Hurricane Flora, one of the worst hurricanes of the twentieth century, laid waste to much of Cuba in 1963, Castro seemed to be everywhere. He bailed out flooded fields, helped to rebuild schools and risked his life in rescue efforts. The 1970 harvest fell short of its 10-million tonne target by 1.5 million tonnes, but 'The Maximum Leader' was out in the fields with his machete and, with a typically Fidel gesture, he got the entire staff of the Soviet embassy out in the fields as well.

Ever the sportsman, Fidel shares Cuba's passion for baseball.

* * * SUMMARY * * *

- From the earliest days of the Cuban Revolution, real power lay with Fidel Castro himself.

- In late 1961, Castro declared himself to be a Marxist-Leninist, giving a clue about the direction in which he would lead the country.

- Marxism-Leninism adopts the ideas of pure Marxism but calls for a core of revolutionaries to act and rule on behalf of the working masses.

- This idea that individuals directly affect history appealed to Castro's character and his own understanding of major leaders throughout history.

- Castro linked anti-American sentiment with Cuban patriotism to build support for the revolutionary government.

- While becoming friendly with America's chief Cold War enemy, the Soviet Union, Castro strove to turn this friendship to Cuba's advantage.

- Following the Soviet example, more and more of Cuba's overall planning became the responsibility of the central government.

- Castro tried to concentrate on certain problem areas – such as education, health and land ownership – one at a time and each year took on the title of its particular issue.

- Cuba's sugar crop and its links with the Soviet Union lay at the heart of the country's economy and Castro tried hard to increase annual harvests throughout the 1960s.

- Although Cuba began to assume a Soviet-style Marxist appearance, Castro remained determined to stress the specifically Cuban nature of the Revolution.

- Travelling widely through the country and joining workers, Castro aimed to lead by example.

7 International Involvement

No matter what gains Fidel Castro has achieved in his own country, he has become an international statesman because of his reputation in the world community. Despite – or even because of – Cuba's long-standing rift with the United States, it has been an example for many Third World countries. Castro has recognized this from the earliest days of the Revolution. Cuba's future and his own personal standing have been entwined with events beyond the shores of his own island. Over the years, his efforts to support other revolutionary movements have made headlines around the world. These actions not only served to unsettle the United States. At times they even threatened Castro's relationship with his chief ally, the Soviet Union.

THE FOOTSTEPS OF BOLÍVAR

KEY FACT

The Liberator

Simón Bolívar (1783–1830) was the principal leader in the struggle for South American independence from Spain. He was born into a wealthy family in Caracas, Venezuela, on 24 July 1783. Bolívar fought in a revolt against the Spanish in Venezuela in 1810. The rebels were defeated by the Spanish royalists, and Bolívar was forced to flee the country. Two years later he led another expedition to Venezuela, capturing Caracas in 1813 and becoming dictator. Royalist forces defeated him again in 1814, and he went into exile in Jamaica and later Haiti.

Uniting his forces with those of other Venezuelans and European volunteers, Bolívar again invaded Venezuela in 1817. He established a revolutionary government and was elected president. In 1819, Bolívar's army crossed the Andes to end Spanish rule in what is now Colombia. Bolívar dreamt of a united Spanish America, and in the early 1820s he helped gain independence for the lands that would become Ecuador, Peru and Bolivia (which took its name from his own). His efforts to govern the different countries proved impossible and he was forced to hand over power in 1830, the year in which he died. Nevertheless, he is still remembered as 'The Liberator' and his birthday is a national holiday in Venezuela and Bolivia.

Castro's hero José Martí was only one in a long line of Latin American revolutionaries. Nearly a century before Martí's insurrection, the peoples of many South American countries rose up against Spain. Local rebel fighters made their names in the various countries, just as Marti would later in Cuba, but one name stands out among this group of anti-colonial soldiers: Simón Bolívar. Responding to the calls for independence and justice throughout South America, Bolívar mobilized popular support and ended the hated Spanish rule.

Having overthrown the Batista regime in his own country, Castro saw parallels with the events of the Bolívar era. The great Latin American earned his title 'The Liberator' by linking the struggles of the individual nations. He was an internationalist. Bolívar saw how the injustices of the separate colonies against Spain were similar. Looking at the South America of the mid-twentieth century, Castro saw that once again the various peoples shared hopes and grievances. Wealth was concentrated in the hands of a few, and most ordinary people found it hard to find work let alone afford health care and education. Might not the example and support of revolutionary Cuba help these nations overthrow their regimes and set up similar governments?

Castro's relationship with his friend and political ally Che Guevara during this period was important. In a way, each represented a different side to the same issue, even if they agreed on fundamentals. This difference was evident in their views on how Cuba should be governed. Che, always a romantic, believed that society should be organized according to the communist slogan: 'Each must give according to his capacity and receive according to his needs.' Castro, showing a more realistic approach, preferred: 'Each must give according to his capacity and receive according to his work.' He defined this version as socialist – as opposed to communist. Che believed that Cubans would work hard simply because they had a moral duty to make the Revolution succeed. Payment, like other things in society, should be equal. Castro, on the other hand, could see that the public would soon protest at such a system. Who could stand by and watch as the government paid the same to a worker who loaded ten tonnes of cargo as it did to one who loaded 20? Castro might have shared Che's ideal in this respect, but he was realistic enough to see it as just that – an ideal – rather than a basis for government policy.

A different side of the same debate – romantic versus realistic – would re-emerge within the subject of other revolutions in Latin America. Che, an Argentine who had already left his own country to help another (Cuba), believed that all Latin Americans deserved to experience what Cuba had achieved. For him, revolution was a mission that would only be finished when all of Latin America – and later, all of the Third World – had overthrown their capitalist governments. Castro shared this ambition to a degree, and he certainly supported the idea of further revolutions in Latin America, but once again, it was a pragmatic, realistic concern that lay behind his thinking. Castro's main concern was Cuba, and it made sense that if Cuba had a number of fellow revolutionary governments in the region, then his own country would benefit. Cuba would then need to rely less on the Soviet Union, and it would enjoy a wider chance to trade with other countries. Moreover, future revolutionary governments would probably become regional military allies.

Revolutionary movements, similar to the 26 July Movement in Cuba, had developed in several South American countries by the time Castro had assumed power. Both Fidel Castro and Che Guevara were eager to export their ideas, but by the time Cuba and the Soviet Union had become close, it was clear that Castro's ally did not support such 'unofficial' revolutionary activity. The Soviet Union preferred to support local communist parties in Third World countries, rather than revolutionaries who might not co-operate so closely with Moscow. Still, Castro went ahead with his plans. Cuba's first aid, as early as 1959, went to the National Liberation Front in Algeria, which was fighting for independence from France. Che himself went to Africa in 1963, but returned disillusioned with the tribal squabbling within various revolutionary groups that he visited.

THE DEATH OF CHE

Africa would once more occupy Castro's thoughts, but the more local, Latin American revolutionary groups became his real concern. Once more Che was to be Cuba's unofficial ambassador to the groups in Venezuela, Colombia, Bolivia and elsewhere. He seemed more fitted to the role of agitator than administrator, and his efforts to modernize Cuba through the Ministry of Industry had become bogged down by the mid-1960s. In 1965, he left Cuba in mysterious circumstances, leaving behind a farewell letter in which he abandoned Cuban citizenship.

Castro read Che's letter to a stunned meeting of the Cuban Communist Party, but after that Che's name was not mentioned in public. In fact he endured a dogged struggle to stir up revolution in Bolivia, which had seemed ripe for rebellion. Che faced the opposition of the Soviet Union and the local communists. His efforts failed to kindle any widespread local support and on 9 October 1967 he was killed in an ambush. Recently revealed information suggests that the Bolivian military had been tipped off by the communists.

Fidel Castro announced Che's death to a stunned Cuba. His Jesus-like image, now familiar throughout the world through T-shirts and posters, appeared all over Cuba as his legend grew. Castro had lost one of his closest allies and friends, but in some ways Che's death strengthened Castro's position. Che had never shied away from criticizing the Soviet Union's lack of 'internationalism' and he had also accused Moscow of treating Third World countries in an imperialist fashion. This voice was now stilled. Cuba had a revolutionary martyr, but one who would never again create trouble between Fidel Castro and the Soviet leadership.

THE AFRICAN EXPERIENCE

The cause of Latin American revolution was dearest to Fidel Castro's heart, but after Che's death he concentrated on building relations with the governments of these countries. In the early 1970s, South America had an elected Marxist government (in Chile) as well as left-wing reformers in senior positions in other countries. If friendship and good trading relations could develop on these terms, then Castro the realist saw no immediate need to stoke the revolutionary fires there.

As for a successful, Cuban-style Revolution, Castro believed that the best hopes actually lay in Africa. Despite the internal disputes that had so discouraged Che Guevara in 1963, there were many thriving revolutionary movements. Castro kept track of these and through the 1960s set up military missions in Algeria, Ghana, Congo, Guinea, Somalia and Tanzania. On 3 May 1972, Castro left Cuba for a two-month trip to ten countries on two continents. The brunt of the trip was in Europe, where the Cuban leader visited the Soviet Union's Eastern European allies and then held a series of high-level talks with the Soviet leadership itself. Before reaching Europe, Castro spent about two weeks in Africa, building personal contacts and setting the stage for deeper Cuban involvement there. Guinea's President, Ahmed Sekou Touré, introduced the Cuban leader to a cheering crowd with the words: 'Cuba is the light in Latin America.' Castro responded to the crowd's enthusiasm there and in his later stops in Sierra Leone and Algeria. He abandoned his usual military fatigues in favour of local dress – a white tunic or a flowing robe, depending on the occasion.

Algeria, with its revolutionary socialist government, was a planning centre for revolutionary activity on the continent. Castro was briefed about the various movements as well as Africa's distaste for the apartheid system of government in South Africa. Within three years Castro would be able to translate his support for African revolution into concrete action. The spur came in April 1974 when Portugal's new left-wing government announced that its African colonies would be freed the following year. One of these colonies, Angola, had three rival factions waiting to assume power. One was backed by the United States, while another looked to South Africa for support. The third, the Marxist MPLA, already held the capital Luanda. Castro promised to support the MPLA.

By late 1975, thousands of Cubans were pouring into Angola to help defend the MPLA. There were Cuban doctors, teachers and engineers, but the largest group were soldiers. Some 300,000 Cubans eventually served in Angola. Others would see fighting in Ethiopia, where Castro hoped to support the Marxist government of Colonel Mengitsu Haile Mariam in its struggle with neighbouring Angola.

The Soviet Union was very pleased to have Castro furthering its interests in these African conflicts. Gone were the disputes about whether or not a revolution was 'unofficial'. Both Moscow and Havana agreed on which groups to support. Moreover, the bulk of Cuba's African soldiers were themselves Afro-Caribbean. They could integrate into the local population in a way that Soviet troops could only imagine.

Some Africans saw Cuba's involvement as a betrayal of its own revolutionary past. Somalia's government was similar to that of Cuba in the early 1960s and its rivals in Ethiopia were the sort of pro-Soviet government that Che Guevara had once criticized. Other Third World countries saw Castro as being too close to Moscow. Despite these criticisms, Cuba became a leading member of the Non-Aligned Movement, a group of Third World countries that aimed to steer clear of close attachments to either of the superpowers. Castro's powerful speeches and simple force of character had helped him gain influence within the Non-Aligned Movement. His aims might have mirrored those of Moscow, he argued, but his actions proved the value of Third World co-operation across borders and even continents. By the end of the 1970s, Fidel Castro had become chairman of the Non-Aligned Movement. He had become the unofficial spokesman for the Third World.

✵ ✵ ✵ SUMMARY ✵ ✵ ✵

- Fidel Castro has always been aware that his reputation depends on his international standing as much as his image in Cuba.

- Both Castro and Che Guevara admired the nineteenth-century freedom fighter Simón Bolívar, who dreamt of a united Spanish South America.

- Castro and Guevara differed, as they did on several other major issues, on how revolution could succeed in Latin America and elsewhere.

- Castro, unlike Che, adopted a realist approach and based his support for revolution on how it would benefit Cuba and whether it would upset the Soviet Union.

- Che Guevara left Cuba secretly in 1965 to stir up Latin American revolution but was killed in Bolivia two years later.

- Che's death made it easier for Castro to side with the Soviet Union in foreign affairs because Che had often been critical of Moscow.

- In the 1970s, Castro turned his attention to Africa, where he felt that revolutionaries had the best chance of succeeding.

- From the mid-1970s, Castro was sending thousands of Cuban soldiers to support Marxist governments in Angola and Ethiopia.

- Despite Castro's closeness to the Soviet Union, he rose in importance within the Non-Aligned Movement and became its chairman in 1979.

Fighting for Survival 8

The last year of the 1970s – as if to mark the twentieth anniversary of Cuba's Revolution – seemed to offer Fidel Castro real cause to celebrate. In 1979, Havana played host to a summit of the Non-Aligned Movement, attended by 92 heads of state or their representatives. It seemed as if every strand of political and religious belief was represented. The world leaders included Marshall Tito, Yugoslavia's veteran communist leader, as well as the deeply religious Muslim leader of Pakistan, Mohammad Zia ul-Haq. Indian Prime Minister Indira Gandhi, herself a member of a legendary family of statesmen, was also present. Presiding over the whole affair, entertaining guests and showing off his country's achievements when he was not making long speeches, was Fidel Castro himself.

Political events nearer home also seemed to be playing into Castro's hands. That same year, 1979, saw another successful revolution in Latin America. A group of Marxist guerrillas known as the Sandinistas had seized power in Nicaragua, a Central American neighbour of Cuba. Even closer to home, in the Caribbean, there was another new ally. The popular lawyer and politician Maurice Bishop, a close friend of Castro, had established a Marxist-leaning government on the tiny island of Grenada. With Castro's international reputation at an all-time high and with new allies settling into place in the region, it seemed that things were looking up. Or were they?

CARIBBEAN CONCERNS

The rebel victory in Nicaragua was particularly gratifying for Fidel Castro because it echoed his own earlier triumph in so many ways. The Sandinistas, like Castro's 26 July Movement before them, had used guerrilla tactics in their struggle while they built popular support in the countryside. Their uniforms were based on the Cuban design and their slogans resembled those used by the Cuban guerrillas two decades earlier. The Sandinista commander, Daniel Ortega, made no secret of the assistance and inspiration provided by Fidel Castro's Cuba.

Castro, for his part, was eager to build links between the two countries based on a personal bond between their leaders. Ortega had been in power only a month when he accepted Castro's invitation to review Cuba's troops on Cuba's national day (26 July), the twentieth anniversary of the Revolution. Castro in turn visited Nicaragua several times in the first year of Sandinista power. In his wake came thousands of Cubans – doctors, nurses, teachers, engineers and military advisers – who were eager to help their new comrades. As he did in the 1970s, when Cuban troops were dispatched to Africa, Castro stressed that these Cubans were volunteers. Once more, he added, Cuba was proving its unique qualities by being the only Third World country prepared and able to offer assistance to another one.

Cuba, however, was careful not to send troops into Nicaragua. Castro knew that the United States would interpret this as a threat and would possibly respond by attacking not just Nicaragua but Cuba itself. His caution was well placed because a belligerent mood had swept across the United States. Ronald Reagan, elected president in 1980, was a conservative whose foreign policy was to put America's interests in the forefront. He had a popular following both in the US Congress and among the American people generally. Reagan's view of the world was clear-cut. America and its allies needed to guard the world against the evils of communism. US–Soviet relations became more jittery as the United States spent more and more on military equipment. More than two decades later, some analyst's believe that Reagan's stance helped to end the Cold War.

President Reagan detested the Sandinistas almost as much as he hated Castro and he took a personal interest in shaping US policy towards Latin America. Under Reagan, the United States pumped millions of dollars into the region, mainly to arm and support the anti-Sandinista guerrillas known as the Contras (the nickname was Spanish shorthand for **counter-revolutionaries**). Reagan also aided the governments of El Salvador and Colombia in their long-running conflicts with Marxist guerrilla groups.

Castro believed that he was dealing with the first US President since the Bay of Pigs who might well be inclined to invade Cuba. More than once in the early 1980s, President Reagan threatened to 'go to the source' of Central America's upheavals. The source, in Reagan's view, was undoubtedly Cuba. Castro recognized the danger and built up his army and civilian guards – just in case. Castro's concerns grew more intense in 1983 when the United States invaded Grenada. Maurice Bishop's Marxist government had been a source of irritation to the Americans, particularly when Grenada invited Cuban engineers to expand their tiny airfield. In a move that many of America's staunchest allies compared with David and Goliath, US marines landed and took control of the island. Out went Grenada's experiment with Marxism. The hundreds of Cuban technicians and labourers, considered military personnel by the Americans, were sent packing.

Once more Castro could claim the moral high ground as the victim of 'Yankee' bullying, but no amount of diplomatic sympathy could provide Fidel Castro with the security he needed more than ever. He redoubled his efforts to build a defensive force and by the mid-1980s there were more than a million Cubans – ten per cent of the population – ready to bear arms if their island faced invasion. All of this, of course, was proving costly for a small country with not much more to export than sugar.

THE CRUMBLING KREMLIN

By the mid-1980s, Fidel Castro faced troubling concerns from another, previously unexpected source – the Soviet Union. Cuba's major ally was entering a troubling phase. Unsettling protests were brewing up in its nearest neighbours, the communist countries of Eastern Europe. The first sign of trouble had erupted in 1980 in Poland, where shipyard workers in Gdansk had established the Solidarity trade union – an illegal action in the eyes of the pro-Soviet government. Despite some heavy-handed police tactics, and even the imposition of martial law, the Polish government had been forced to recognize the deep support that Solidarity enjoyed among the Polish people. Some of the strictest communist restrictions were eased during this time, measures that were echoed in several other European communist nations.

The Soviet Union itself saw very few demonstrations but it entered some uncharted territory. There, in the heart of the communist world, the changes came not as a result of any mass movement but from the **Kremlin** itself. In March 1985, Mikhail Gorbachev became the head of the Soviet Communist Party, the most

KEYWORD

Kremlin: the head-quarters of Russia's (and formerly, the Soviet Union's) government in Moscow.

powerful position in the Soviet Union. Like the reformers of Eastern Europe, he recognized that poor management, limited human rights and outdated working practices were damaging his country. He responded by reshaping the Communist Party so that it could respond to the people's needs. The key words in Gorbachev's programme were *glasnost* ('openness') and *perestroika* ('rebuilding').

Fidel Castro visited Moscow in 1986. Banners and headlines proclaiming the new strategy were everywhere, and the public speeches of Soviet leaders urged the people to fall in step with the new order. Privately these same leaders tried to convince Castro that he should also follow their example. Despite Castro's independent spirit and his high profile in the Non-Aligned Movement, he knew better than to defy Moscow. Any plans he had for Cuba depended on maintaining the economic lifeline that had been in place for nearly four decades. This dependence had reached a point where Cuba was costing the Soviet Union $12 million a day.

UNCHARTED WATERS

Cuba had dabbled with some reforms of its own in the early 1980s, although nothing on the scale that Gorbachev and his Kremlin colleagues were proposing. Castro had allowed a small amount of private business to reappear in Cuba. Private taxis were permitted in Havana and in other large towns and cities. Farmers were allowed to sell some of their crops in the open market. These experiments were localized and small-scale and the overall economy – farming and industry in particular – remained unchanged. Returning from his Soviet trip in 1986, Castro adopted some of the *glasnost* elements of the new-style Soviet approach. He prided himself on his rapport with the people, even if he was seen less often riding through the countryside and canvassing opinion. Cubans were encouraged to criticize ministers, but there was no outlet for any real dissent about the overall running of things.

It is not surprising that Castro was half-hearted about transforming Cuba along Gorbachev's lines. He could foresee, correctly as it turned out, that opening up the Communist Party fully would lead to its unravelling. Too much reform would destroy the whole communist system in a country. After his brief flirtation with *glasnost* Castro began to criticize the Soviet leader. By the time Cuba was preparing for the 30th anniversary of the Revolution, there was a stubborn new slogan in place: 'Socialism or Death'.

As Fidel Castro saw it, the writing was on the wall. As a shrewd observer of world events, he knew that the end was in sight for the Soviet Union if it continued on the path of reform. He was not prepared to risk his own secure power base by copying that strategy, especially if it left him weakened if – or in his view, when – he lost his chief ally. In a forceful speech to the 1986 Congress of the Cuban Communist Party, he announced a series of measures known as the Rectification Campaign. If Cuba was to remain secure in a post-Soviet future, it had to return to basics. Castro attacked corruption and materialism within Cuba, which he saw developing from the slight economic reforms that had been under way. It was time to find the motivation that had guided Cuba in the early days of the Revolution. That meant recalling the moral values of the early 1960s, when people had been prepared to make sacrifices. He called for more production and volunteer work, coupled with less consumption. Castro was determined that his cherished system would survive, even if it meant going it alone.

The 1980s, which had begun so promisingly for Cuba, ended with some of Castro's dire predictions beginning to come true. In 1989, Cuba signed a 25-year friendship treaty with the Soviet Union, but the trade terms spelt out a new relationship. Soviet aid to Cuba was set to be cut dramatically. Even more alarming was the news that the famous sugar-for-oil deal would continue but on terms that no longer favoured Cuba. Castro had a glimmer of hope when anti-reform communists tried to topple Gorbachev from power in 1990, but it was short-lived. Gorbachev returned briefly, only to be replaced by Boris Yeltsin. An even keener reformer than Gorbachev, Yeltsin oversaw the dismantling of the communist system. In 1991, the Soviet Union ceased to exist. Russia, Ukraine and the other republics that had comprised the Soviet Union became independent. To rub salt into Castro's wounds, they looked to Washington for aid and economic advice as they sought to rebuild their countries – without communism.

✳ ✳ ✳ SUMMARY ✳ ✳ ✳

- The 1980s started well for Fidel Castro with two neighbouring countries – Nicaragua and Grenada – forming Marxist governments.

- Castro formed personal friendships with the leaders of these countries and encouraged Cuban volunteers to help in the fields of medicine, education and engineering.

- The United States, under President Ronald Reagan, adopted a fiercely anti-communist position and spent millions to topple the Nicaraguan Marxist government.

- US troops invaded Grenada in 1983, ridding the island of its Marxist government and causing Castro to believe that Cuba might be next.

- Cuba's main ally, the Soviet Union, fell in step with the calls for reform that had swept through Eastern Europe's communist nations in the mid-1980s.

- On a trip to Moscow in 1986, Fidel Castro saw the new spirit of reform in action and made some similar, but short-lived reforms when he returned to Cuba.

- Castro predicted accurately that offering too much reform would destroy Soviet communism, so he called for stricter rule – and more sacrifices – in Cuba.

- A 1989 treaty with the Soviet Union promised 25 years of friendship but it offered less favourable terms for trading sugar for oil.

- Even that treaty became worthless in 1991 when the Soviet Union abandoned communism and then disbanded, leaving Castro without his staunch ally.

9 Dealing with Uncle Sam

One of the cherished legacies of Spanish rule in Cuba is the magnificent architecture. Imposing Baroque and **neo-classical** buildings line the palm-fringed boulevard that follows the curve of the harbour. The plaster and paintwork on most of these buildings have peeled and cracked, but the overall effect is still magical. *Habañeros*, or natives of the Cuban capital, take pride in their city, which is preserved as a UNESCO World Heritage Site.

KEYWORD

Neo-classical: an architectural style of the eighteenth and nineteenth centuries that uses columns and arches in the style of classical Greek and Roman architecture.

This imposing seafront would be the romantic first impression for anyone arriving by ship. Once ashore, the visitor would notice two unusual elements, each of which is as characteristic of the city as its colonial architecture. The first is the number of billboards and signs with the word *Yanqui* and featuring either a shifty Uncle Sam or a greedy, cigar-chomping businessman – and sometimes both. The second is the array of cars on the uncrowded city streets. Long-finned Pontiacs and Buicks, Chevrolets and Cadillacs, Havana's cars resemble props from an American film of the 1950s. In fact, these treasured vehicles do date from the 1950s, representing the last decade during which American cars were imported to Cuba. The supply of cars – and just as importantly, spare parts – stopped abruptly when the United States broke off all trade links with Cuba soon after Castro assumed power. Ingenious mechanics manage to do repairs with anything they can find – bits of farm machinery, rubber hosing and even string.

These first impressions actually tell a lot about American influence over the past century, and this influence continues despite a 40-year rift. Lying no more than 70 miles away at its closest point, the United States is a presence that Cuba cannot disregard. Fidel Castro has certainly never ignored the United States. Nearly every move he makes is calculated to have some effect on the giant to the north. Sometimes appeasing, often provocative, his words and actions are

KEYWORD

Contradictory: representing two opposite points of view.

carefully chosen. He knows that the Cuban people have strong memories of America's bullying behaviour over the years, and the Uncle Sam posters usually serve to rally popular feelings of independence. The image of plucky little Cuba, which has stood up to the mightiest superpower for more than four decades, has an appeal far beyond Cuba, but Castro also recognizes that there were more than four decades of close relations between the two countries. Those well-tended Cadillacs are proof enough of the affection that many Cubans have for the United States. The Cuban leader must balance these seemingly **contradictory** attitudes. It is like walking a tightrope – but since the fall of the Soviet Union there has been no net.

FACING THE EMBARGO

Right from the beginning of Cuban independence, the United States created conditions in which its companies could thrive in Cuba. By preventing Martí and his freedom fighters from entering Havana and dictating the terms of their own independence, the United States gave itself a military and political role to play in Cuba. It was not shy about using the military option in the early decades of the twentieth century, but from the 1940s its role was largely economic. In the period between the end of World War II and the fall of Batista in 1959, the United States enjoyed an economic boom. Increased prosperity translated into greater investment in foreign branches of American companies. With bribery and corruption built into the Cuban political system, these companies were able to increase their influence even further.

By the late 1950s American companies controlled:

✳ 90 per cent of Cuba's mines;

* 80 per cent of its **public utilities**;

* 50 per cent of its railways;

* 40 per cent of its sugar production;

* 25 per cent of its bank deposits.

> **KEYWORD**
>
> Public Utilities: businesses that perform an essential public service (such as electricity, gas or water supply).

Fidel Castro, even during his time as a guerrilla in the Sierra Maestra mountains, knew that Cuba would suffer badly if the Americans 'pulled the plug' on all these investments. At that time he was proud of his growing reputation as a popular hero and leader-in-waiting. The American public, which had no particular fondness for the Batista government, warmed to the larger-than-life rebel. This feeling continued even after Castro had seized power. In April 1959, just three months after toppling Batista, Fidel Castro visited the United States as a guest of the American Society of Newspaper Editors. He got enthusiastic receptions at Princeton and Harvard universities, where the students cheered his passionate speeches. In New York, he made a point of visiting the black district of Harlem, proclaiming his solidarity with the people there and calling for 'bread without terror' and 'revolutionary humanism'.

Then things began to go sour very quickly. It was one thing for Americans to support revolutionary idealism in theory, particularly when the theorist is a striking young man with fire in his eyes. It was quite another thing when some of Castro's economic measures began to take hold. One of his first moves was to nationalize the Cuban Telephone Company as a way of reducing phone charges. The company, however, was owned by the American communications giant ITT. Other companies, such as the American-owned oil firms discussed earlier, were nationalized. Quite simply, Fidel Castro was bad for business. What was worse, he was growing closer to the communist system of the Soviet Union.

Voices in the United States called for the overthrow of this dangerous revolutionary. Secret government meetings discussed how this could be done. A full-scale invasion was ruled out at that stage, but the United States considered assassination or simply economic isolation. Despite the momentum developing against Castro, some influential Americans warned against isolating Cuba and sending it into the Soviet camp. One of these was the respected American journalist Walter Lippmann, who wrote in his column: 'the thing we should never do in dealing with revolutionary countries, in which the world abounds, is to push them behind an iron curtain raised by

KEYWORDS

Subverted: having one's character changed by another person or way of thinking.

Covert: secret (usually referring to government actions).

Paramilitary: referring to an armed organization that operates in place of a regular military force.

ourselves. On the contrary, even when they have been seduced and **subverted** and are drawn across the line, the right thing to do is to keep the way open for their return.'

Unfortunately for Castro, and Cuba, Lippmann did not have the ear of those in power in the United States. In 1960, US President Eisenhower approved a **covert** action plan to overthrow Castro. Backed up by a 'powerful propaganda campaign' that set up an anti-Castro radio station, the plan ended all sugar purchases and oil deliveries. As a background to the ill-fated Bay of Pigs invasion, the Americans also began organizing a **paramilitary** force of Cuban exiles to invade the island.

All of these measures were linked to the trade embargo that the United States imposed in 1960. Like the rusty, slightly worn Cadillacs on Havana's streets, the economic relationship between the two countries has remained largely unchanged for more than 40 years. An occasional 'thaw', such as the tentative diplomatic efforts in the mid-1970s, would just as quickly 'freeze' as the United States registered its disapproval of, for example, the Cuban military presence in Africa. Throughout this long period, Fidel Castro has preferred to use the more powerful word 'blockade' to describe America's embargo.

CROSSING THE WATER

Not allowing goods and services into Cuba was just part of the complicated relationship that developed between Cuba and the United States. Every bit as important has been traffic in the opposite direction – human traffic. More than a million Cubans have fled their homeland since Castro came to power; nearly all of them settled in or around Miami, Florida.

In one way, this steady exodus has been a profound embarrassment for Fidel. Losing ten per cent of the population is not a ringing vote of confidence. On another level, however, Castro has succeeded in making a virtue out of a necessity. Most of the people who fled Cuba in the early days were from the privileged business or professional classes. These were people who had lost out – or stood to lose out – as private property was confiscated and companies were nationalized. Educated and articulate, they posed a real threat to the regime if they were to remain in Cuba. Letting them leave released pressure on the Cuban leader. These departures affected Fidel Castro directly. In September 1965 he announced that anyone who wanted to leave was free to go. Thousands of people turned up at the tiny port of Camarioca. Among them were two of Fidel's sisters.

IN THE SPOTLIGHT

The flow of Cubans from their homeland has gone largely unnoticed by the world's press. Two incidents, however, did grab international headlines. Together they illustrate the scale and the emotions raised by this flow of people. The

KEYWORD

Asylum: safety and protection.

first came in April 1980 when 10,000 Cubans stormed the Peruvian embassy in Havana seeking political **asylum**. Angry mobs, loyal to the government, attacked them and Castro denounced the would-be émigrés as 'scum' in his annual May Day speech. The United States responded by offering a home to all of the Cubans. Castro agreed and then emptied jails of thieves and mentally unstable prisoners. An exodus of Cubans, eventually numbering 125,000, left the port of Mariel and sailed to Florida. Castro had used his 'pressure release' tactic once more and he had extra satisfaction when he learned of a crime wave in Miami at the end of the year.

The second incident involved only one person, an eight-year-old boy named Elian Gonzalez. He had joined his divorced mother and other family members on a boat heading for Florida in 2000. The boat was hit by a storm and only the boy survived. He was taken to relatives in

KEYWORD

Federal: (of the United States) operated by the central government.

Miami but the Cuban authorities protested that the boy belonged back in Cuba with his father. Passions on both sides of the argument grew and the confused little boy became a symbol of the whole Cuban–American crisis. A series of court cases in the United States finally decided that he should be allowed to go back to Cuba. In April 2000, **Federal** law enforcers broke into his relatives Miami house in a dawn raid and forcibly took Elian away. Several days later, still looking confused by it all, he arrived back in Havana for a tearful reunion with his father. Also present was a tall, bearded man who embraced the reunited family. By becoming involved at every stage of the dispute, Castro had taken the disrupted family and turned it into a symbol of Cuba's whole nation. Traitors, scum and criminals were free to leave the country, but Castro would fight to the last to retrieve a true son of Cuba.

❋ ❋ ❋ *SUMMARY* ❋ ❋ ❋

- A first-time visitor to Cuba today would notice evidence of the country's lingering preoccupation with the United States.

- Fidel Castro recognizes the Cubans' contradictory feelings towards their huge neighbour – fearful anxiety and longing to resume closer relations.

- Since the beginning of the twentieth century, the United States shaped independent Cuba into a country that would welcome its companies.

- On the eve of the Revolution, American companies or their Cuban branches controlled a large portion of the overall Cuban economy.

- Castro was a popular leader with many Americans before and shortly after the Revolution.

- The American backlash, leading to an economic embargo and even an invasion, began with secret plans to overthrow Fidel Castro after he took over many American companies.

- More than a million Cubans – one tenth of the population – have left the island since Castro came to power in 1959.

- Fidel Castro permits this exodus because it rids the country of potential rivals, critics and others he sees as a threat.

- The flow of refugees from Mariel in 1980, which included many criminals, was the largest single departure of Cubans.

- Fidel Castro took a personal interest in the plight of Elian Gonzalez in 2000 to show that he would protect the rights of Cubans to remain on the island.

The Man Behind the Beard 10

Fidel Castro welcomed a special guest to Havana in December 2001. Gerry Adams, the leader of Northern Ireland's Sinn Fein political party, had arrived to dedicate a plaque honouring **IRA** hunger strikers who had died 20 years before. The meeting produced a ripple of interest in the British and American Press because of some recently disclosed IRA links with Cuban-sponsored guerrillas in Colombia. Sinn Fein has always relied on support from Irish-Americans, who have no love for Castro.

Apart from the formalities and the recent guerrilla scandal, the meeting was interesting for another reason. The two bearded figures in Havana were familiar faces at the time of the hunger strikes. Each had entered the 1980s facing a new set of uncertainties: Sinn Fein and the IRA dealing with the steadfast opposition of UK Prime Minister Margaret Thatcher and Castro up against the fiercely anti-communist President Ronald Reagan. Faced with his challenge, Adams has spent the past two decades steering his party (and eventually, the IRA) away from violence and towards political involvement in problem-solving. Castro, on the other hand, chose not to follow the Soviet Union's example of reform and has the distinction of being one of the very few leaders of a Marxist government as the world enters a new millennium. To see the results of his recent journey we must look behind the public face of Cuba and its leader and look at what drives Fidel Castro.

CASTRO'S PERSONAL LIFE
Castro's image, however much it has been reworked by the man himself, remains powerful. The Maximum Leader still dresses and carries himself like the young guerrilla fighter of the 1950s. The beard

is his most recognizable 'prop'. He explains that he and his fellow guerrillas found it too much trouble to shave while they were waging their war in the Sierra Maestra. While acknowledging that 'the beard became a symbol of the guerrilla', Castro explains to Havana newspaper readers why there is a practical reason to retain it decades later. 'If you calculate 15 minutes a day to shave, that is 5,000 minutes a year spent shaving.' That time could be better spent reading or exercising. Despite this justification, Castro has always discouraged other Cubans from wearing guerrilla beards. So it would seem that he prefers to think of his own in symbolic terms.

Some elements of this image have long since vanished, but live on in the public imagination. One of these is his trademark cigar, which even figured in some of the CIA's suspected assassination plans. Despite the importance of tobacco to Cuba's economy, the government mounted an anti-smoking campaign (on health grounds) in the early 1980s. Interviewed in December 1985 for Brazilian television, Castro announced that he himself had given up smoking. The disclosure was startling, and soon became a lead story in television news broadcasts and newspapers around the world. True to his character, though, Castro achieved it on his own terms: 'If someone had forced me to quit, I would have suffered … but since I forced myself, it worked.'

The combat fatigues, the beard and the cigars are all part of the public image that has been built up of Fidel Castro. The private life of the Maximum Leader is less well known. His marriage in 1948 to Mirta Díaz-Balart lasted five years. Mirta tired of Fidel's total devotion to politics but the end came when Fidel, in prison after the Moncada raid, learned that Mirta had been working for the Batista government. Castro never remarried although he has had a string of relationships with beautiful women. His deepest affection was for Celia Sanchez, whom he had known since the 1950s. The two were an unofficial couple until her death in 1980. Since then there has been no long-term companion for Castro.

Fidel Castro loves good food and by all accounts served some excellent meals while he was in prison in the 1950s. Dignitaries visiting the presidential palace in Havana dine on freshly caught lobster and other seafood, washed down by aged Cuban rum. A luckier few join Castro on Cayo Piedra, a tiny island off the southern coast. There Castro can enjoy his favourite sport of underwater fishing and the lobsters served at Cayo Piedra are often caught by the host himself. Castro is said to be good company and – although some people might be surprised – he is an excellent listener. After-dinner conversations range across an array of topics and the Cuban leader is well informed on most subjects. When the guests retire, Castro often spends hours at his desk working on and reworking his speeches. He has an almost poetic command of Spanish, which explains why people will willingly listen to him speak for hours on end.

REAL INDEPENDENCE

Fidel Castro's cherished hero José Martí fought for Cuban independence, but he could only manage a half-measure. The settlement reached between the United States and Spain after the Spanish–American War ensured that Cubans would not have a full say in conducting their own affairs. The dependence on the United States became one of the targets of Fidel Castro and his fellow guerrillas. They were proclaiming humanity and justice as their ideals, but they also felt that Cuba needed to be fully independent to achieve these goals. And yet in no time Cuba plunged into another relationship with a superpower sponsor, the Soviet Union. Castro abandoned some of his original ideas, such as support for other Marxist guerrilla movements, in order to please the Soviets. When the Soviets liberalized their economy in the 1980s he also followed suit, although half-heartedly. The mighty dollar had been replaced not by the rouble (the internationally worthless currency of the Soviet Union), but by the Soviet oil that Cuba received in exchange for its sugar.

With Soviet aid, Castro built the foundations of his own version of Marxism, and despite Castro's prominence in the Non-Aligned

Movement in the 1970s, many neutral observers still considered him to be a Soviet puppet. In a sense, it was only in 1991 that true independence arrived on Cuba's shores. The nation faced the new decade without the Soviet Union, and with a dwindling number of fellow Marxist states anywhere in the world. The country faced economic collapse without the prop of the sugar-for-oil deal that had supported Castro for so long.

Rather than cave in to pessimism, Castro sent the country into its Special Period in Time of Peace. In essence, it was an attempt to shore up the gains of the Revolution in the time of crisis. Castro imposed harsh restrictions on food and fuel supplies, while insisting that the people consider reverting to the horse and wagon to harvest sugar, if fuel supplies ran so low. Cuba suffered, with its once-respected health record put under strain. The same country that outdid the United States in infant mortality rates in 1987 was, by the mid-1990s, facing acute food shortages and widespread malnutrition.

Castro was forced to open up the economy in a way that he had shunned during the years of *glasnost* in the Soviet Union. More drastic – and unexpected – was the move to legalize possession of US dollars in 1993. That meant that Cubans could benefit directly from money sent by their relatives in the United States. Then, Castro loosened the suffocating restrictions on private enterprise. Farmers, taxi drivers, restaurant operators and a number of other categories were now allowed to do something that many Cubans had never even heard about – make a profit. So, with a modest profit-making economy in operation, Castro felt he could promote Cuba as a tourist destination. He argued that foreign visitors could marvel at the achievements of the Revolution, while Cuba benefited from the injection of foreign cash. With typical determination, Fidel pushed tourism firmly once he decided on this course of action. By the end of the 1990s, Cuba had more tourist beds than the rest of the Caribbean region.

THE PAPAL VISIT

Religion is one of the areas where Fidel Castro has run into trouble over the years. Cuba has traditionally been a Roman Catholic country, a legacy of Spanish rule. Catholic clergy had the main role in educating Fidel himself, and he has long admired the fiercely intellectual Jesuit order. But religious beliefs and Marxist theory

KEYWORD

Opiate: a drug that dulls the senses and makes its users satisfied to day-dream rather than perform any actions.

do not usually mix. Marx had described religion as the '**opiate** of the masses', referring to the way in which working people would endure injustice and hardship on Earth as they awaited heavenly paradise.

Most religious denominations face severe restrictions in Marxist countries, and post-revolutionary Cuba was no exception. Catholics were forbidden access to top government jobs and they were forbidden to join the Communist Party. The Catholic Church, for its part, was critical of Fidel Castro and his 'godless' regime. Catholic clergy found themselves detained on trumped-up charges in Cuba, and those in American exile have often been at the forefront of anti-Castro protests.

So it came as a surprise to many people that Fidel Castro warmed towards the Church in the 1990s. Open-air masses attracted thousands of worshippers and anti-religious restrictions were lifted one by one. These measures set the stage for a most unlikely event – the visit by Pope John Paul II in 1998. To no one's surprise, the Pope called for greater personal freedom in Cuba, but he then turned to the subject of the American embargo, which he denounced as misguided and wrong. Castro swallowed the criticism but it was a small price to pay for the Pope's other comments.

GRAND OLD MAN OR DINOSAUR?

Now in his fifth decade of power, Fidel Castro qualifies as few others do as an 'elder statesman'. It would have taken enormous force of character for anyone to take a poor country with one major crop and to turn it into an example for more than half the world. Castro has done just

Pope John Paul II and Cuba's Maximum Leader exhanged views during the papal visit of 1998.

that, and by highlighting the strategic significance of his island he has grabbed the attention of two world superpowers. Trying to sail his own course between their conflicting demands, he has rebuffed and outlasted the other.

Will these same skills be as useful in the twenty-first century? The answer seems to be 'yes', at least on the evidence of the first years. Tourist income has helped boost the economy and some of the new industries that Castro encouraged during the Special Period – notably biotechnology and medical technology generally – look set to grow in the future. Castro probably takes more pride in the fact that even in the darkest hours of the Special Period, Cuban spending on health (average life expectancy is 75 years), education (class sizes average 26) and welfare (everyone is entitled to a pension) increased. If Fidel Castro could manage this during a real crisis, then he can feel confident about the future.

Cuba celebrates the centenary of its independence in 2002. Fidel Castro's speeches dwell on the pride and the self-determination of the Cuban people, contrasting conditions now with the US-dictated terms of 1902. The subsequent decades of coups, takeovers, infighting – and free elections – ended on 1 January 1959. On that New Year's Day, did the Cuban people swap one military dictator for another, more powerful, one? Or did they cast aside corruption and inequality and embark on a journey towards a glittering future? That is up to the Cubans themselves to decide. Their Maximum Leader is sure he has the answer.

* * *SUMMARY* * *

• Fidel Castro knows that his public image has become an important symbol of Cuba itself.

• Castro argues that his beard is a common-sense way of saving time, but he discourages other Cubans from growing beards.

• Contrary to popular opinion, Fidel Castro no longer smokes cigars, having quit in the mid-1980s.

• After his marriage to Mirta Díaz-Balart ended in divorce, Castro never remarried although he has had many relationships with women.

• Castro established the Special Period in Time of Peace to deal with the crisis after the fall of the Soviet Union.

• Cubans gained a measure of freedom to own businesses in the 1990s.

• Pope John Paul II visited Cuba in 1998 and called for an end to the US trade embargo.

• Fidel Castro remains confident that the Cuban people will share his belief that their recent sacrifices will bring about a better future.

Chronology of Important Dates

1926	Fidel Castro is born (13 August) on his father's estate near Santiago in eastern Cuba
1945–50	Attends Havana; graduates with a law degree
1947	Joins new Ortodoxo party
1949	Marries Mirta Díaz-Balart (divorced 1954)
1952	Former president Fulgencio Batista overthrows Cuba's civilian government
1953	Leads rebel attack on military garrison at Moncada, near Santiago (26 July)
1953–5	Captured and jailed on the Isle of Pines
1955	Released from jail (15 May) Castro goes into exile in Mexico (7 July) to plot overthrow of Batista's government
1956	Rebel force led by Castro lands in Cuba on the yacht *Granma* (2 December)
1957	Makes Sierra Maestra mountains the rebel stronghold after initial victory at La Plata (17 January). *New York Times* interview (17 February) widens awareness and appeal of the 26 July Movement
1958	Unsuccessful army assault on rebels in Sierra Maestra (May–August). Public, business and military support sways from Batista who flees Cuba (31 December)
1959	Castro enters Havana in triumph (8 January); becomes prime minister (17 February); visits United States (April); announces agrarian reform (8 May)
1960	Cuba and the Soviet Union build ties and announce a sugar-for-oil trade deal (June); US President Dwight Eisenhower imposes trade embargo on Cuba (13 October)
1961	US-backed Cuban invaders defeated Cuba at the Bay of Pigs (17 April); Castro proclaims himself a Marxist-Leninist (1 December)

1962	Soviet missiles withdrawn after the Cuban Missile Crisis (22–28 October)
1963	Castro visits the Soviet Union and is warmly received
1967	Che Guevara executed in Bolivia while trying to spread Marxist revolution in South America
1970	Cuba fails to meet the 10-million-tonne sugar harvest target set by Castro
1972	Castro visits Africa, Eastern Europe and the Soviet Union (May and June)
1975	Cuban troops sent to aid MPLA fighters in Angola, staying for 13 years
1979	Castro presides over the conference of the Non-Aligned Movement in Havana (August); welcomes Sandinista rebel victory in Nicaragua
1980	Mariel Boatlift (21 April to 26 September) sees more than 100,000 Cubans migrate to United States with the permission of the Cuban and the US governments
1983	United States invades Marxist-governed Grenada and expel Cuban engineers
1986	After visiting Gorbachev's Soviet Union Castro initiates some limited economic reforms based on *glasnost* and *perestroika*
1989	As the Soviet Union unravels, Castro announces motto of 'Socialism or Death' to strengthen Marxist control of Cuba
1991	Soviet aid to Cuba ends and Soviet Union itself disbands (December); beginning of Special Period in Time of Peace
1998	Pope John Paul II visits Cuba and meets Castro
2002	Castro presides over Cuba's centenary of independence.

GLOSSARY

accomplice   a person who knowingly helps someone else in a crime

agrarian   referring to farming and agriculture

arsenal   a weapons storehouse

asylum   safety and protection

baroque   a style of ornate art and architecture that was popular in Europe in the sixteenth and seventeenth centuries

blockade   either an actual blocking of ports by armed ships or a ban on trade with a particular country

blueprint   the basic plans for a grand design

Bogota   the capital of the South American country, Colombia

bourgeois   a Marxist term of abuse, referring to excessive devotion to private property

bureaucratic   (of an organization) operating with a rigid system of rules and procedures

cabinet   a group of senior political aides who help shape government policy

Cadillac   an expensive American car, seen as a symbol of wealth

civil rights   basic human freedoms for example, of speech, the right to vote and worship and to have education and health care

constitution   the written code of laws that limits the power of a country's government

contradictory   representing two opposite points of view

co-operative   a farming or business group in which people pool their talents and skills and share any profits from goods they produce and sell

cornerstone   the load-bearing stone of a building and, by extension, the most important principle of an argument or set of beliefs

counter-revolutionary   someone who tries to reverse the actions of a revolution

coup   a government takeover, often by force

covert secret (usually referring to government actions)

debacle an action that is a complete failure

defector someone who leaves a country to live in that country's main enemy country

denunciation a public criticism

embargo a government order prohibiting trade

entourage a group of followers

elite representing the minority of society that has the best advantages (of wealth, education, etc.)

Federal (of the United States) operated by the central government

garrison a group of soldiers stationed in an armed building

Great Depression the period in the 1930s when many countries faced economic hardship

guerrilla a member of a band of soldiers who use ambush and surprise attacks rather than full-scale open battles

Hannibal a general* (247–183BC), of ancient Rome's enemy Carthage, who crossed the Alps and invaded Italy

IRA (the Irish Republican Army) a paramilitary group that has used violence to end British control of Northern Ireland

junta a group of military leaders who govern a country, usually by force

Kremlin the headquarters of Russia's (and formerly, the Soviet Union's) government in Moscow

liberate to set free

machete a broad-bladed knife used to cut down sugar cane and other vegetation

manifesto a public statement of beliefs

market value the price that something could fetch if it were sold freely

Marxist representing the political ideals of Karl Marx (1818–83)

May Day 1 May, the most important holiday in Marxist countries as it celebrates labour

menial　lowly and sometimes degrading

militia　a body of citizens enrolled for military service

neo-classical　an architectural style of the eighteenth and nineteenth centuries that uses columns and arches in the style of classical Greek and Roman architecture

opiate　a drug that dulls the senses and makes its users satisfied to daydream rather than perform any actions

paramilitary　referring to an armed organization that operates in place of a regular military force

pragmatic　realistic and common-sense

profit sharing　a system of business that allows all of a company's employees to benefit when the company does well

public utilities　businesses that perform an essential public service (such as electricity, gas or water supply)

radical　favouring drastic and wide-ranging changes

rhetoric　the ability to use language effectively

subverted　having one's character changed by another person or way of thinking

tribunal　an organized meeting to decide on the fate of someone

unanimously　in complete agreement

BIBLIOGRAPHY AND FURTHER READING

Bay of Pigs Peter Wyden, Simon & Schuster, New York, 1979

Castro Sebastian Balfour, Longman, London, 1995

Castro's Daughter Alina Fernandez, St Martin's, New York, 1998

Castro's Final Hour Andres Oppenheimer, Simon & Schuster, 1992

Cuba and the Politics of Passion Damian J. Fernandez, University of Texas Press, Austin, 2000

Cuba and the Revolutionary Myth Fred C. Judson, Westview Press, Boulder, Colorado, 1984

Cuba between Reform and Revolution Louis Perez, Oxford University Press, 1988

Cuba from Columbus to Castro Jaime Suchlicki, Brassey's, New York, 1998

Diary of the Cuban Revolution Carlos Franqui, Viking Press, New York, 1980

Episodes of the Cuban Revolutionary War Ernesto 'Che' Guevara, Pathfinder, New York, 1996

Fidel Peter Bourne, Dodd, Mead, New York, 1986

Fidel: A Critical Portrait Tad Szulc, Hutchinson, London, 1987

Fidel and Religion Talks with Frei Betto, Havana, 1987

Fidel Castro Clive Foss, Sutton Publishing (Sutton Pocket Biographies), Stroud, 2000

Fidel Castro Robert E. Quirk, Norton, New York, 1993

Fidel Castro Nothing Can Stop the Course of History (Interview with Jeffrey Elliot and Mervyn Dymally), José Martí Publishing, Havana, 1985

Fidel Castro and Company, Inc. Manuel Urrutia Lleo, Frederick A. Praeger, 1964

Guerrilla Prince: The Untold Story of Fidel Castro Georgie Anne Heyer, Little Brown, Boston, 1991

Revolutionary Cuba Terence Cannon, José Martí Publishing, Havana, 1981

Six Days in Havana James A. Michener and John Kings, Souvenir Press, London, 1990

INDEX